THE QUILTER'S ALBUM
OF
BLOCKS & BORDERS

THE QUILTER'S ALBUM OF BLOCKS & BORDERS

JINNY BEYER

ILLUSTRATED BY
JINNY BEYER AND DAN RAMSEY

EPM
PUBLICATIONS, INC.

EPM Publications, Inc., 1003 Turkey Run Road, McLean, Virginia 22101

Printed in the United States of America

LIBRARY OF CONGRESS CATALOGING IN PUBLICATION DATA

Beyer, Jinny.
    The quilter's album of blocks & borders.

    Bibliography: p.
    Includes index.
    1. Patchwork—Patterns.   2. Quilting—Patterns.
I. Ramsey, Dan, 1945-   .   II. Title.   III. Title:
Quilter's album of blocks and borders.
TT835.B44   1986   746.9′7041   86-4262
ISBN 0-914440-92-6 (pbk.)

Illustrations by Jinny Beyer and Dan Ramsey

Design by Gerard A. Valerio

CONTENTS

From *Godey's Lady's Book*, Volume 39, July, 1849.

Because this book is an effort to begin documentation of many of our quilting patterns, I wish to dedicate it to all those people, impossible to name, who developed the art of quilting. Though their patterns were handed down from one generation to another, the identities of the quiltmakers all too often were lost in time.

Some of those anonymous quilters come to life in the following poem. It was found clipped in a scrapbook kept by Lena Wetherbee who was born during the Civil War. The identity of the poem's author fortunately was preserved, but not the date or the name of the newspaper in which it appeared. It conveys appreciation not only for the old patterns but for the women themselves who created and stitched them.

SUNNING QUILTS
BY
EFFIE SMITH ELY

Out from their scented chests I draw
And hang my bright quilts in the sun,
Fashioned by deft and patient hands
Whose work-days now are done.

This Irish Chain in vivid rose
Was Great-Aunt Phoebe's hope and pride—
Dear little girl, who died too young
To be a happy bride.

These colors, with fair stitches joined
To form a bold True-Lovers' Knot,
Were lame Aunt Miriam's—in their glow
Her dull days she forgot.

My strong grandmother, unto whom
Life brought most bitter grief and smart,
Piecing this flower basket learned
To mend a broken heart.

Dead kinsfolk, who have left to me
These quilts you made in vanished springs,
Would that I had your fortitude
Your joy in simple things!

I wish to thank all of those people who gave me permission to use their designs in this book. Special thanks go to Cuesta Benberry who generously shared information that she has been compiling for years on the history of quilt patterns.

INTRODUCTION

This book has four purposes: to present a catalog of square geometric designs for use in quiltmaking and other crafts; to classify these designs into the categories set forth in my previous book, *Patchwork Patterns*, for easier identification and drafting; to offer a guide to the use of fabric; and to include a section on border designs that responds to the renewed interest in medallion quilts and elaborate borders.

Most of the square designs are traditional ones which have been used by quiltmakers over the years; I have tried, nevertheless, to give a source for each design. Listed first are the earliest date and name I could document for a particular pattern, followed by all other names given to the same pattern. In addition to traditional patterns, I have presented several new designs made by today's quiltmakers as a further effort to provide both a date and source for quilt blocks. The maker's name appears beneath each of the new patterns. To the best of the designer's knowledge and my own, these are original; however, it is entirely possible that someone else has created the same design. I do not mean to slight anyone, and if a design has also been done by someone else, omission of that person's name is due simply to the fact that I was unaware.

THE QUILTER'S ALBUM
OF
BLOCKS & BORDERS

Lone Star, antique quilt, ca. 1920. Photographed by Steve Thompson.

SOURCES FOR QUILT PATTERNS

I t is common knowledge that many of the quilt patterns in use today were also used during colonial times. The designs were passed down from mother to daughter, carried in covered wagons to be shared with newfound friends, traded at fairs, or obtained from a traveling peddler. Those patterns and their names that reflected hard times, the beauties of nature, religious dedication, political tides, patriotism, and the pioneering spirit have become part of our nation's folklore. As quilt patterns spread to other parts of the country, or as basic designs were colored in different ways the names were often changed.

In this book, I feel it would be repetitious to show each pattern with every color variation and the name attributed to it. The real importance of a design lies in the individual treatment; it should be made to please its maker rather than compulsively copied. Quilting is a distinctly personal art form that can be perpetuated not only through the creation of new designs but also in the interpretation and execution of the old. Therefore, I have taken a basic design—regardless of how it is "supposed" to be colored—and put it together as I might if I were sewing the block. I have listed all the names I found for any particular design. It may be difficult to recognize some of the patterns—even familiar ones—because they can look so very different according to the way in which they are colored.

As a part of my research into quilt patterns, I tried to find the oldest listing for each design in a book or periodical. The name of a pattern, as it appeared in the oldest source, is listed first along with the source and date. Other names found in later publications, but given to the same design, are listed subsequently in alphabetical order. At times the old periodicals failed to give a name to a printed design. If such was the case, it is listed as "Godey Design" or "Peterson Design" with the next oldest name following that and the remainder in alphabetical order. My study is by no means complete, but at least it is a beginning.

Sources for Quilt Patterns

In my attempt to document quilt designs, I spent many delightful hours at the Library of Congress thumbing through fragile pages of *Godey's Lady's Book, Peterson's,* and numerous other beautiful old books and magazines. It is difficult, however, to find periodicals before the 1830's, so most of my work reflects material from 1830 on.

After scanning roughly two centuries' worth of publications for articles pertaining to needlework, I began to gain both perspective and insight into the trends and ideas of days gone by. I also began to form an opinion regarding the importance of quiltmaking to the women of the nineteenth century, or perhaps I should say, to the literature of that period. My view was probably slanted because most of the periodicals undoubtedly were prepared with the city woman in mind. The hard-working pioneer women on the frontier had totally different needs.

I reached the general conclusion that, from the second quarter of the nineteenth century until the 1890's, quiltmaking flourished; however, it was usually considered unworthy of mention in the news-papers and magazines. In contrast to "fancy" work, the making of a quilt was considered "plain" and—at least in the minds of those who wrote the books and periodicals—fit only for old women who could no longer see to do finer work, for children who were just learning to sew, or for the poor who had to salvage anything usable. Any mention of patchwork usually referred to its being made from silk, which perhaps elevated it somewhat from "plain" to "fancy." Rarely were quilts, as such, mentioned—only fancy pincushions, seat covers, throws, or other decorative items which could also be pieced in silk.

Godey's Lady's Book was one of the best sources of quilt patterns for the women of the nineteenth century, or so I had been told. There-fore, in my search for articles and illustrations of patchwork designs, I looked there first. What I discovered was quite a revelation. I found only one quilt pattern in this magazine from its inception in 1830 until 1850. That pattern was for a hexagon design which we call Grand-mother's Flower Garden, but which was referred to in the January 1835 issue as Honeycomb, Six-sided, or Hexagon patchwork. To my surprise, the article was written especially to appeal to young girls rather than adults. "Little girls often find amusement in making patchwork quilts for the beds of their dolls, and some even go so far as to make cradle-quilts for their infant brothers and sisters."[1]

In those first years of publication, decorative embroidery patterns were the types of needlework most frequently shown. Several patch-work designs were introduced during the twelve-year period from 1850 to 1862, but the manner in which they were presented seemed almost apologetic. It was apparent that the editors could scarcely believe women were amusing themselves in such an insignificant way, and that they hoped the majority of their readers who were primarily interested in fancy work could forgive their brief digression to such a menial form of needlework. The articles were not about *quilts* but were concerned

[1] *Godey's Lady's Book,* January 1835, p. 41.

with decorative patchwork. In 1850 when the first patterns were presented, the accompanying text read:

"Many improvements may be made in the old style of patchwork that we have been accustomed to see, and, in anticipation of some improvement in the designs at present used, we venture to intrude a few remarks, trusting that our *'Family Friends'* will not take them amiss." [2]

"As a change from the accustomed routine of knitting, netting, or crochet, the production of ornamental patchwork will be found an agreeable variation." [3]

It is interesting to note that when various designs were published in the periodical, few of them were named. In fact, most periodicals did not assign names to the designs until sometime in the 1890's. For the most part designs followed the overall mosaic style, and the only descriptions of how to patch spoke of what we now refer to as the English method of piecing over paper. With one exception, patterns for the designs were never given—only pictures. Obviously, it was assumed that women knew how to draft, cut out, and piece the patterns. Perhaps patchwork was so common that it was unnecessary to explain how to do it—just as today no instruction is needed to sew on a button. Any mention of patchwork seemed to indicate how easy it was.

In referring to the elaborate border design pictured below, the March 1860 *Godey's Lady's Book* said:

Godey Border Design, *Godey's Lady's Book,* 1860

"Patchwork has especially established for itself the character of a winter industry, as it requires no additional light for its execution, the work which produces it being slight and easy. The only care which it exacts is a mathematical precision in the foundation shapes of which it is composed, and a knowledge of the laws of colors: that is, light and shade, and contrast. When these two points are remembered and practised in the arrangement of patchwork, most ornamental effects may be produced. We this month give a border which we think will prove very satisfactory to those ladies who may feel tempted to execute it." [4]

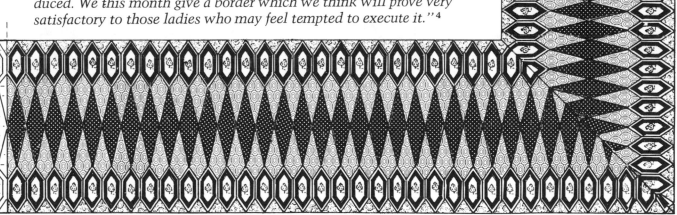

After a short-lived interest in patchwork during the middle of the nineteenth century, *Godey's Lady's Book* again turned its attentions to embroidery, netting, crochet and knitting.

[2] *Godey's Lady's Book,* April 1850, p. 285.
[3] *Godey's Lady's Book,* March 1851, p. 198.
[4] *Godey's Lady's Book,* March 1860, pp. 262-263.

Sources for Quilt Patterns

Disappointed by the lack of information about quilting and patchwork given during the sixty years of this magazine's publication, I searched through other books and periodcals from the nineteenth century. All seemed to parallel the Godey attitude about quilting, so consequently, I found very little information. Most references that I did come across discussed only silk and decorative patchwork; piecing with cotton seemed to be looked down upon. *The Dictionary of Needlework*, published in 1882, stated: "Satin, silk, and velvet Patchwork is used for cushions, hand-screens, fire screens, glove and handkerchief cases, and pincushions; cloth Patchwork for carriage rugs, couvrepieds [foot coverlets], and poor peoples' quilts."[5]

Further support of this attitude may be found in *The Lady's Manual of Fancy-Work*, in which Mrs. Pullan discusses patchwork:

> *"This is a favorite amusement with many ladies, as by it they convert useless bits of silk, velvet or satin, into really handsome articles of decoration. Of the patchwork with calico, I have nothing to say. Valueless indeed must be the time of that person who can find no better use for it than to make ugly counterpanes and quilts of pieces of cotton. Emphatically is the proverb true of cotton patchwork, Le Jeu ne vaut pas la chandelle! It is not worth either candle or gas light."*[6]

Ah, Mrs. Pullan, if only you could see the tattered silk remains of so many quilts and articles of decoration today and compare them with their still sturdy counterparts made of cotton! You might wish to withdraw your proverb about cotton patchwork for it is obvious that the fragile fabrics "cannot hold a candle" to tried and true cotton.

The significant factor in nineteenth century literature about patchwork and quilting is the *lack* of information. It is curious that there are so many more examples of beautiful quilts from the 1800's which attest to the heritage of this fine art than there is mention of it in the literature. What does exist supports my opinion that quilting was not highly regarded except as a lesson for young girls or a pastime for the old who no longer had the keen eyesight necessary for "fancy" work.

It seems that by the middle of the nineteenth century, the days of the old-fashioned quilting bees were gone. In 1849 T. S. Arthur wrote an article for *Godey's Lady's Book* entitled "The Quilting Party." In it he reminisced about the good old days:

> *"Our young ladies of the present generation know little of the mysteries of 'Irish chain,' 'rising star,' 'block work,' or 'Job's trouble,' and would be as likely to mistake a set of quilting frames for clothes poles as for anything else. It was different in our younger days. Half a dozen handsome patchwork quilts were as indispensable then as a marriage portion; quite as much so as a piano or guitar is at present. And the quilting party was equally indicative of the coming out and being 'in the market' as the fashionable gatherings together of the times that be.*

[5] S. F. A. Caulfield and Blanche C. Saward, *The Dictionary of Needlework*, An Encyclopedia of Artistic, Plain and Fancy Needlework, p. 379.
[6] *The Lady's Manual of Fancy-work*, 1859, p. 95.

As for the difference in the custom, we are not disposed to sigh over it as indicative of social deterioration. We do not belong to the class who believe that society is retrograding, because everything is not as it was in the earlier days of our life history. And yet—it may be a weakness; but early associations exercise a powerful influence over us. We have never enjoyed ourselves with the keen zest and heartiness, in any company, that we have experienced in the old-fashioned quilting party . . . . . Ah, well! More than twenty years have passed since then. The quiltings, the corn-huskings, the merry-makings in the village of M--- are not forgotten. Twenty years. How many changes have come in that period!" [7]

The *Hearth and Home Newspaper* had a column called "Mrs. Kate Hunnibee's Diary." In the June 4, 1870 issue, this column mentioned quilting and gave a pattern for the "Square A" design. The article, which follows, indicates that quilting was not uncommon for women of that time. However, it also gives the impression that the older women, with their fond memories of the days of the "bees," were usually the ones who did needlework of this type; otherwise, quilts were made by a group for the poor or by a frugal housewife who felt it necessary to put her scraps to good use.

"May 23rd

Sewing-Circle this afternoon at the Parsonage. The parlor, the library, and the dining-room were full, and the ladies all busy with fingers and tongues. It would have been difficult to tell whether more talking or sewing were done. One of the young ladies sat at the sewing-machine in the dining-room, and kept it running—now stitching the hem of a skirt, now sewing up the body of a shirt, or hemming a ruffle for a night-wrap or a pillow-slip. But the centre of attraction was in the parlor, where the old ladies, who used to go to 'quilting-bees' when they were girls, sat around the big quilting-frame which belongs to the Society, with every now and then a young lady sandwiched in between them to thread their needles . . . . . As the frame belongs to the Society, the various members have the use of it whenever they wish, and we have found it a great convenience every fall in preparing our annual barrel for the home missionary, to whom we always send a quilt and a comfort or two . . . . . There was quite a discussion among the ladies in the library about patching quilts.

Mrs. Knox—I think it is as good a way to teach little girls how to sew as we can find. They may thus learn to arrange colors with taste, and cut out by patterns with exactness. Let them make doll-baby quilts first and then piece a big quilt for themselves. I have one now that I began to piece almost as long ago as I can remember, made in my childhood, and I wouldn't take any money for that quilt. My mother—dear old lady— takes my calico pieces and scraps of muslin as they accumulate, and busies herself in putting them into blocks or stars or fancy patterns for me.

Mrs. Lester—But it always seemed a great piece of folly to me to buy calico for the express purpose of cutting it in pieces that it may be sewed together again. For my fancy, white marseilles spreads and rose blankets are more tasteful, less burdensome as a covering, and more agreeable than quilts and comforts.

Mrs. Blake — But if one has pieces enough in the house — and most everyone has — it is certainly a good plan, in hours of leisure, to put them in so enduring and useful a form as a quilt. I have a box in which every thing of this kind is kept, and from which I make the little girls that come to see me presents for their dolls' toilettes and bedding." [8]

Other articles I found substantiated my idea that in the second half of the nineteenth century quiltmaking seemed to be a pastime for the very old or the very young. In "Patchwork" from the 1857 *Godey's Lady's Book*, Ellen Lindsay describes patchwork done as a child and then:

". . . until we go forward to the old grandmother, who finds patchwork the finest work her aged eyes and trembling fingers will permit her to undertake . . . an old lady, an aunt of mine, one of the single sisterhood, is constantly making the most beautiful patchwork quilts . . . but the prettiest piece of work I almost ever saw was a quilt made by an old lady friend for her first grandchild . . ." [9]

And in 1877 S. Annie Frost stated about patchwork:

"Although this work seems to come more under the heading of plain than fancy needlework, this little book would scarcely be complete were all reference to it be omitted. It is generally our first work and our last — the schoolgirls' little fingers setting their first crowded or straggling stitches of appalling length in patchwork squares, while the old woman, who can no longer conquer the intricacies of fine work, will still make patchwork quilts for coming generations." [10]

The idea that quilting is for old ladies seems to have carried over into this century. How often have we heard such phrases as, "Oh, look at that. My grandmother used to quilt," or "I can remember all the old ladies at the church doing quilting." Often when I go before a new group to lecture, they are shocked that I am not an older woman. All of which causes me to wonder just how far around the world the notion that quilting is for old ladies extends. I kept telling a friend of mine from India about my quilting and he never quite understood. Then one day he came to my house and I eagerly brought out my quilts. He was horrified. "You mean *this* is what you are doing? But that is what the *old* women in the villages do at home!"

In the 1890's quilt patterns began to appear more abundantly in the magazines and newspapers and, for the first time, names were regularly attached to designs. They were no longer called simply "mosaic," "a pretty patch," and so forth. The Ladies' Art Company, founded in the 1880's by a German immigrant family, specialized in commercial quilt patterns. Their catalogs of quilt designs, available in the 1890's

---

[8] *Hearth and Home Newspaper*, "Mrs. Kate Hunnibee's Diary," June 4, 1870.
[9] *Godey's Lady's Book*, Ellen Lindsay, "Patchwork," February 1857, pp. 166-167.
[10] S. Annie Frost, *The Ladies' Guide to Needlework, Embroidery, etc.*, 1877.

and on into the twentieth century, appear to be the first of any kind to gather together a large number of quilt patterns in one publication. The early copies contained about three hundred patterns which were added to in subsequent printings, until in 1928 there were some five hundred thirty designs.

Most of the books written in the twentieth century have relied heavily on this catalog for quilt patterns. I have a copy of the 1898 *Ladies' Art Company Catalogue,* sent to me by Cuesta Benberry, and it is the oldest source I can find for most of the patterns in this book. She also sent me a copy of the Clara A. Stone catalog, *Practical Needlework,* circa 1910, which has some delightful patterns, many of which I have not seen in any other books old or new. This would indicate to me that the latter catalog was not well circulated since much of it is certainly worthy of further notice. Some of Mrs. Stone's designs are presented in this book.

From the 1920's to the 1940's, interest in quilting seemed to reach its peak. *The Kansas City Star, The Rural New Yorker,* and many other newspapers and periodicals throughout the country published numerous quilt patterns. "Nancy Page" and "Nancy Cabot" columns about quilting were widely read. The majority of the designs presented during this time were not new. Frequently, however, new names were given to the old patterns, most of which had appeared in the earlier *Ladies Art Company Catalogues.* In the 1950's and 1960's interest in quiltmaking or in anything homemade seemed to decline; it was not until the 1970's that patchwork and quilting again saw a tremendous upsurge in popularity. The current revival may even surpass any in our nation's history. Quiltmaking is finally becoming known as something more than just a homey craft or a pastime for the unskilled. Today's quiltmakers can be proud of the new influences they are contributing to this age-old art.

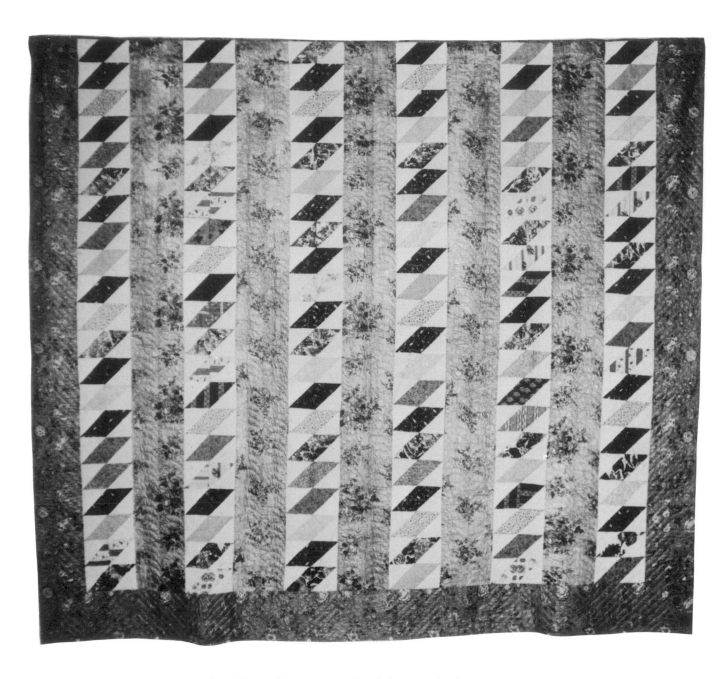

Stripped Border Quilt, antique quilt of chintz and calico, ca. 1810.

THE USE OF FABRICS

The past few years have seen a great change in the way fabrics are used in quiltmaking. It has become apparent that the exclusive use of small prints can create a bland, uninteresting surface; quiltmakers are advancing from the sole use of small calicoes in bright reds, greens, blues and yellows and are moving into an era of sophistication. They have discovered the elegance of larger prints, borders, and more subtle and subdued colors.

This is not a totally new concept, but a rebirth or renaissance of the fabulous quiltmaking that was done in the eighteenth and early nineteenth centuries. What is truly exciting is that modern quiltmakers are not just copying quilts made in the past. They are gathering all of the knowledge learned about quiltmaking during the last two hundred years and are using it to produce even greater quilts than those that were made before.

An important factor in this rediscovery is the awareness that quiltmaking need not be a scrapbag project. Most of us were brought up during the Depression years or right after the war when both goods and the money to purchase them were scarce. Everyone was frugal and the quilts of that time *were* made mostly from scraps. This may be one reason why the so-called Depression quilts are, as a group, less attractive than quilts made during any other time in our nation's history. Those quilts certainly had their share of superb workmanship, but the fabrics and colors used, for the most part, lacked distinction.

I think that the idea that quilts were always made from scraps is a myth. Certainly many of the utility quilts were, but I would wager that equally as many were made by women who carefully sorted through their scraps and then supplemented them with fabrics purchased especially for the quilt, or even bought fabrics specifically for the scrapbag, as we do today. Surely many of the exquisite eighteenth and nineteenth century quilts which we see today were not the result of an accidental use of scraps, but part of a process carefully planned from start to final stitch.

The Orlofskys, in their book *Quilts in America*, state that "by the 1850's materials were bought specifically for the purpose of making a quilt."[1] In describing a beautiful Double Pyramid quilt made in 1819,

---

[1] Patsy and Myron Orlofsky, *Quilts in America.*

Ruth Finley states, "Scraps may have gone into its making, but there was enough of the same material to carry out a premeditated color scheme. In other words, the cloth was cut to suit the quilt, not the quilt to suit the cloth."[2]

The scraps of fabric available to the quiltmaker prior to 1930 blended together far better than those after that period. The dyes were still soft and subtle; there were not a lot of bright, garish colors that clashed with each other. Modern technology not only brought more vivid hues, but fabric was no longer limited almost solely to cotton percale. Crepe, seersucker, blends and double knits began appearing on the market so that today, with such a variety of fabric types and colors available, it is almost impossible to use bits and pieces from sewing projects in our quilts. That is, of course, unless you do as I do. If I am going to make my daughter a dress, I buy only fabric from which the leftovers would be great for quilting.

I inwardly groan when, at the start of one of my beginner classes, a student walks in with a huge bag and beams excitedly, "I have been saving scraps for twenty years and now I am going to learn how to make them all into quilts. I won't have to buy a thing!"

This does not mean that all scraps should be discarded, but that they do need to be carefully sorted and supplemented with other fabrics.

Now that I have had my say about the myth that a fine, well-coordinated quilt can be made from the scraps of fabric accumulated through the years, I want to discuss the type of fabrics to look for and how they can be combined effectively. I want to point out that these are simply my own ideas; the method I use to choose fabrics is not necessarily the only way. It is my hope that you will take these ideas, combine them with knowledge obtained from other sources to enhance your creativity, and produce patchwork that is uniquely yours.

My techniques and ideas are used throughout this book to add textures to the illustrations, and I intend for these designs to serve as an additional lesson in the use of fabrics. Actual study of the patterns should give you more ideas about fabrics than additional chapters on the subject. Color is not included in this explanation. Before color can be considered, I think a basic understanding of the contrasts between light, medium and dark and the size of print used is more important. If these contrasts are not there, then the colors will not work well together.

There are two main points about my use of fabrics: I rarely use solid colors and I do use a border whenever possible.

A few years ago when I was trying to explain why I prefer prints to solids and what I think printed fabrics do for patchwork, I suddenly remembered an incident that had happened to me when I was in the sixth grade. I think it emphasizes the point.

My classmates and I were painting a large mural for the school cafeteria. The design had been drawn and my job was to color all the

[2] Ruth E. Finley, *Old Patchwork Quilts and the Women Who Made Them.*

trees green. Armed with a large brush and a bucket of paint, I began to color the tree tops completely green. Soon a girl friend came up to me and said, "Your trees look like blobs with no life. Instead of coloring them solid green, you should color them in swirls so a little background shows through. Then they will be better to look at." My friend was right. When the mural was finished, the first green blobs I had painted stood out like a sore thumb while the others sparkled and seemed to have movement to them. I think that the same thing occurs in patchwork when solid colors are used as opposed to prints.

The almost exclusive use of prints necessitates very careful selection when placing one print next to another. I have designated names to the different types of prints I use and ones which I avoid.

BUSY PRINTS: These are fabrics that I never buy—or I should say, no longer buy. My fabric boxes still contain some that were purchased when I first began quilting. It was only after much experimentation that I finally realized there are certain fabrics which simply do not work well in patchwork. Of course, my idea of a busy print may differ from someone else's; but to me these are fabrics with too much contrast between stark white or light and dark, too many colors, or too dominant a design. Pieces that have equal amounts of light and dark also tend to be busy because the eye does not have a resting place. Some examples of what I consider busy prints are shown below.

These types of prints may be used but only when combined with a very careful selection of other fabrics. In general, they do not work well with other prints and are used to their best advantage with solid colored fabrics.

SMALL PRINTS: These are prints with a very small design. I like to use some small print fabrics in my work, but I look for a certain type. Rarely do I select a small print that has more than two colors and usually not one that contains stark white. A small print with too many colors is hard to combine with other prints. Fabrics I particularly look for in this category are ones having two shades of the same color—for instance, tan with off-white, brown with tan, navy with light blue,

13

maroon with pink. In general, small prints work best in the tinier patches of a design.

MEDIUM PRINTS: These are fabrics with a print slightly larger than the small. More than two colors is acceptable so long as the print is not too busy. Once again, a stark white fabric with contrastingly dark colors is apt to stand out too much.

Some of these medium prints may appear to look busy because of the regularity of the design; they would look busy if they were used in large pieces. It is important, however, to look at a piece of fabric in terms of what it contains. Many times a print of this sort can be used very effectively by cutting a small square, triangle, or diamond that contains one motif of the design as its center. Thus the fabric takes on a whole new dimension; it becomes quite unlike a larger piece of the same print.

LARGE PRINTS: These are the larger florals, paisleys and chintzes. They usually contain more colors than the fabrics in any other category. These fabrics can be used to fill a large area and are very much more interesting to look at than a solid colored fabric or small print in the same area. Large prints are more attractive when the design has a swirling rather than a symmetrical effect.

SOLID PRINT FABRICS: This is the term that I use to describe fabrics that I use instead of solid colored ones. These prints are not at all busy and from a distance give the impression of a solid color. The little bit of action that takes place simply because they are prints makes them them much more interesting than a solid block of color. In order to have a well-balanced piece of patchwork, one needs to use a solid print. There are three different types of solid print fabrics:

1. The first is a general print that will go with almost anything and can be of medium color.

2. The second type I call background prints. These take the place of muslin or a solid color fabric as the background of a design. These fabrics have to be subtle in both color and pattern in order not to interfere with the main design. Background fabrics can be small or large print so long as they are subtle, soft and the overall effect is of a slightly mottled surface.

3. Very dark solid prints is the name of my third category. This is the last group of solid prints and includes those fabrics that are highly saturated with color. They usually have a solid color background with some sort of design on that, but not a busy design or one that has a lot of colors. Most projects need a very dark fabric of some sort to hold everything together, and one of these dark solid prints can do just that.

BORDER PRINT FABRICS: This term refers to those fabrics from which strips can be cut to represent a border. The use of a printed fabric border can be one of the most unifying factors in a quilt. Border prints fall into two classifications.

1. Regular border prints are those that can be used around a block, around a quilt, or within a patchwork design. They are usually 1½ to 4 inches wide.

 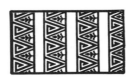

2. Outline borders serve to "outline" or emphasize an area. They are only ½ to 1 inch wide.

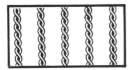 

They should not be confused with or used in place of a regular border. For example, a regular border print can be used as setting strips, or sashing, between the blocks of a quilt, but the outline border is too narrow to separate the blocks effectively. The result looks like an afterthought. (See next page.)

However, the outline border can be used in *conjunction* with the regular border. Each block of the design can be surrounded first with the outline border before the larger border is added as a setting strip. This treatment makes the design even more emphatic.

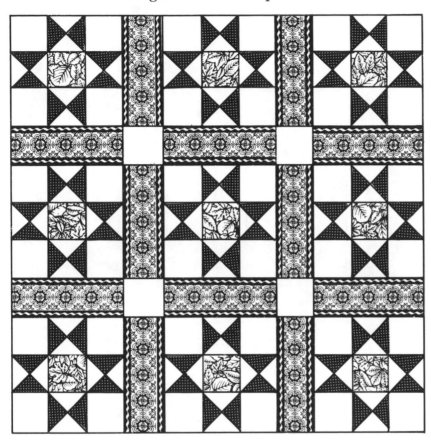

An outline border can also be used to separate a patchwork piece from another piece of fabric, thereby creating a more interesting delineation.

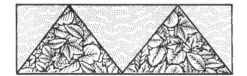 

If the outline border is very dark and appears almost as a solid, it can serve as the very dark accent needed in a patchwork piece.

Combining types of fabrics effectively requires a basic awareness of two things. First, there must be a good balance of light, medium and dark fabrics and, secondly, there must be a balance in the *scale* of prints used. In order to illustrate this point, I have taken the same design and added fabrics to it in different ways. The first two examples show all small prints: in the one on the left, no care has been given to light and

17

dark placement; in the one on the right, a definite concern has been given to contrasts between light, medium and dark.

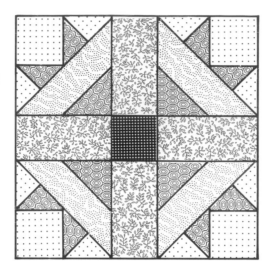 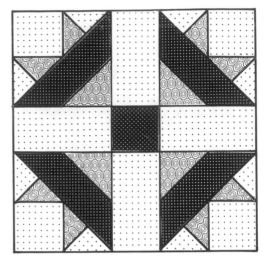

Cross and Crown

The next example shows the use of all large prints with relatively good contrasts between light, medium and dark.

It is apparent that the example using good light and dark contrasts with all small prints shows off the design much better than the one using all large prints; however, the exclusive use of small prints is rather boring. It is at this point that the *balance* between large and small prints becomes *so* important. The next example shows the same design colored with a successful integration of small, medium and large prints, and a relatively good contrast between lights and darks.

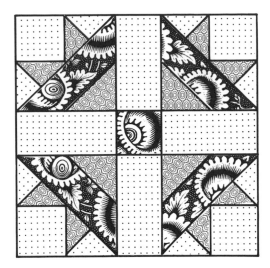

Nevertheless, there is one factor missing in this version and that is the very dark solid print that was mentioned earlier as a *must* for most projects. See how the same design sudddenly comes alive when that dark, unifying element is added.

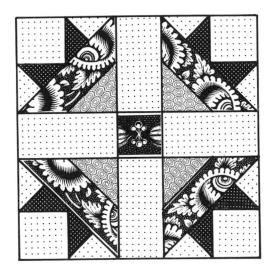

The final step in improving this design is the addition of border fabrics. Whenever a pattern has any straight strips, the perfect opportunity arises to make the pattern more vibrant by adding a border fabric. To illustrate, look at three examples of this design side by side: one with all small prints and good contrast between lights and darks; one with an equally good contrast as well as a balance in the size of the prints; and the last one in which borders have been added. It is obvious that the version with all small prints is boring and the one with borders is the most interesting.

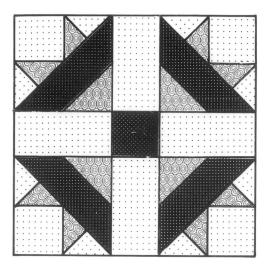

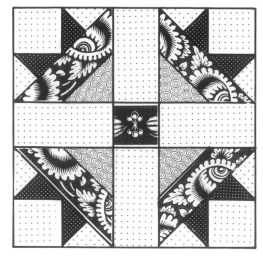

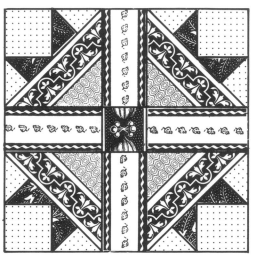

Borders can also be used effectively to create different illusions, as shown in my designs, *Courtyard Square* and *Castle Keep*. The two versions below have no borders. Those on the opposite page show how the use of a border print within the designs can create octagons in the very center and also can give more of a feeling of depth.

Courtyard Square

Castle Keep

20

To make the pattern in the center octagon, great care must be taken to insure that the template for the triangle is centered in exactly the same place on the border fabric each time a piece is cut. I use clear plastic templates, put a dot on the plastic, and then line that dot up in exactly the same place on the print for each piece.

The following are a few more examples showing the difference between using all small prints in a design and using a balance of prints and some borders. I think it is apparent that the group on the right is much more attractive.

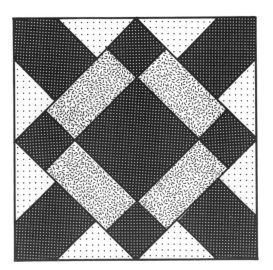 

Fort Sumter

The Use of Fabrics

Greek Cross

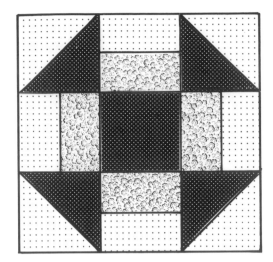 

Roman Cross

Four Corners

In summary, here are some guidelines to follow when putting printed fabrics together:

1. Have a good balance between light, medium and dark colored fabrics.

2. Have a good balance between the size of the prints, using some small, some medium and some large printed fabrics.

3. Use some solid print fabrics.

4. Use a very dark fabric that will hold everything together.

5. If the design is suitable, try using some border fabrics within the design.

6. Stay away from busy prints that have several colors, a sharp contrast in the colors used, or too dominant a design.

7. Larger patches can take a larger print fabric and smaller patches usually are better when made with a smaller print fabric.

COMBINING STRIPS OF FABRICS

The Log Cabin is still one of the favorite designs among quilters, and the string quilting technique has become very popular for making clothing and other quick quilting projects. Both are strip work; they require knowledge of ways to put strips of fabric next to each other effectively. The same principles of using light, medium and dark contrasting colors, and of using different sizes of prints hold true, but further attention must be given to the placement of these various strips.

When geometric designs are used in patchwork, there usually has to be a sharp contrast between fabrics placed next to each other or the design will not be clear. With strip work, however, the opposite holds true. It is not advisable for each strip to stand out markedly; instead, the goal is a subtle blending of the strips. The easiest way to explain this is by looking at the two examples below. Both use exactly the same fabrics, but the one on the right is more attractive than the one on the left. The sole reason for this lies in the order of fabric placement. The example on the left has a strict light-dark, light-dark repetition; whereas, the one on the right shows a blending.

 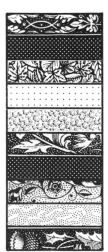

In general, a blending or shading from dark to light and back—where perhaps two darks, a medium, a light and then a medium are placed side by side—is better than a strict light-dark, light-dark placement. Furthermore, a solid print next to a large or medium print is better than two large or medium prints side by side.

To emphasize once again my belief that busy prints are hard to work with, look at the following example to see what happens to the overall effect of the strip on the right, above, when *one* busy print is substituted for one of the other fabrics. I think it ruins the appearance of the entire piece. The same thing can happen when such a fabric is used in a quilt or other patchwork project.

THE PURCHASING OF FABRIC

Finding just the right fabric can be extremely difficult, so I buy fabric when I see one that I like and not necessarily when I have a specific use for it. Otherwise, when the time comes that I need it, chances are the stores will no longer have it in stock.

Fabric manufacturers usually come out with their new lines twice a year, and rarely do they reprint a fabric. Most shops buy only one bolt of each print because of the large investment involved each time the new lines come out. They also want to be certain a fabric will sell before ordering additional bolts. Many times when a reorder is placed, the fabric is no longer available. Consequently, I like to have a good supply of fabric at home so that when I want to start a new project, I have a large selection of materials to choose from and do not have to run around to all the shops hunting for just the right piece. My fabric inventory has grown from filling one cardboard box, to three green plastic trash bags, to a 5' by 8' closet; now I have materials stashed here and there in two other rooms in addition to my closet. I store small scraps in clear plastic sweater boxes, putting a different color in each box; I store large pieces in cardboard storage boxes, once again putting a different color in each box. I use one box just for borders and another just for very small pieces for string work. (As organized as all that sounds, it is usually something of a mess because I get so excited about my next project that I rarely take time to tidy up from my last.)

Very often I am asked, "How much fabric should I buy?" That is a very difficult question. The answer depends on how much is going to be done with the fabric. If plans are to make only one quilt, then you should not buy any more than is needed for that project. If, however, you want to make several quilts and other patchwork items for your home or for gifts, and you feel quilting is going to be a lasting interest, then you would want to build up a nice fabric inventory. When I first started buying fabrics for quilting, I bought quarter-yard pieces. Soon I learned how ridiculous that was because it would all be used up in one project and I would have nothing left. Now, many times I will buy half a yard if it is something I might only use in bits and pieces, here and there. More often, however, if I like the fabric enough, I will buy anywhere from one to three yards, depending on how it might be used. If it is a good background fabric, I will buy five yards or even sometimes a whole bolt. For a good quilt backing I will buy up to six or eight yards.

Buying fabrics with borders is a little different, depending upon how the borders are printed on the fabrics. Some years fabric manufacturers have been kind and have printed a wide range of fabrics that can be used as borders; other seasons there is absolutely nothing. I work on the premise that if I see a border I like but have no immediate use for, I buy it anyway so that when the time comes that I do need it, I will have it. Once I asked a fabric manufacturer's salesman if he had any border prints. He brought out some fabrics that had one border, to be used around the bottom of a skirt. When I explained what I wanted, he said, "Oh, you mean repeat stripes." So now I ask for wide repeat stripes. Of course, it is possible to use the type with only one border; but since it would take between 10 and 12 yards of that to go around the outside of a quilt, the minimum purchase of fabric would be considerable. The amount of repeat stripe or border fabric to buy depends upon how many times the stripe is repeated across the fabric, and how often it will be used in the quilt.

One of my favorites is a double fabric border with a pieced border in between.

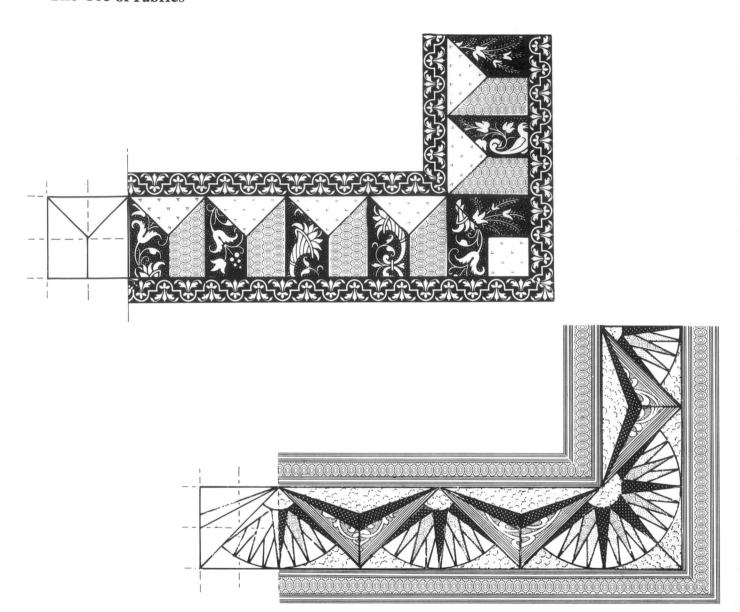

To make these borders will take almost twice as much yardage as going around the quilt only once. Should a piece of fabric have the *same* stripe repeated across the width, then a purchase of three yards, or the length of the quilt, would be sufficient because there would be so many stripes. If, however, the fabric is composed of several different stripes and each one is repeated only three times, then about four yards of fabric would be needed in order to have enough of the stripe to go around the quilt once, or eight yards to go around twice.

If there is absolutely *no* printed border fabric available to buy, then it may be necessary to manufacture one. This can be done by combining fabrics to make them *look* like a printed border. Many overall fabric prints actually appear in repeat units. Perhaps the flowers are printed in rows, or some other design is repeated regularly. It is possible to cut out a straight strip of one of these rows or units and attach another fabric on either side. Sometimes narrow outline stripes are available, and these stripes can be cut apart and then sewn to the sides of a piece of fabric to make a border. Granted, this requires a lot of extra work, but the end result is well worth the effort. Below are some examples of overall fabrics and narrowly striped fabrics that have been combined to make borders.

 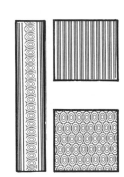 

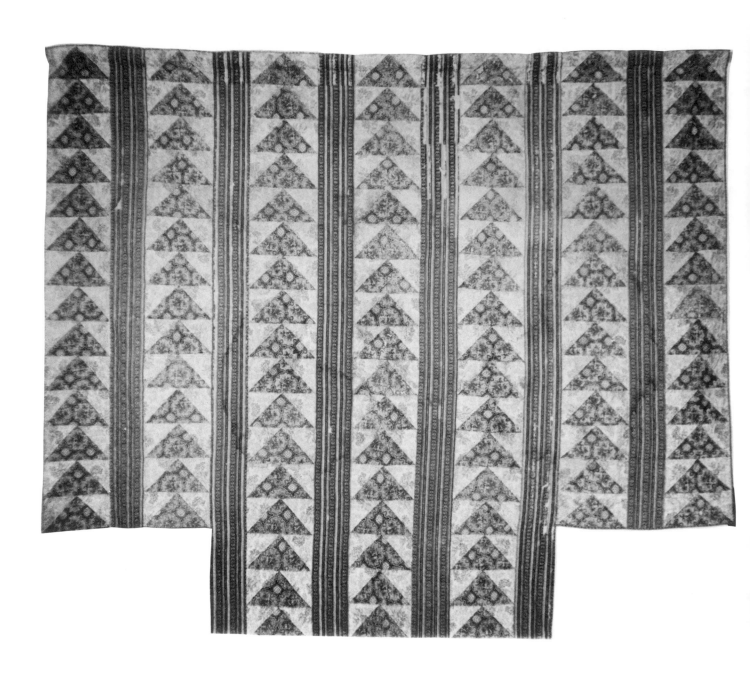

Flying Geese, antique quilt of European chintz and homespun backing, ca. 1800.

III

CATEGORIZING DESIGNS

My last book, *Patchwork Patterns*, set forth the basic categories used in almost all geometric design. It also described in detail the methods of drafting patterns within each category, showing how patterns fall into certain grids and how to draft the various grids. Since most of the patterns within a given category follow basically the same principle, once one has mastered those techniques, it is possible to draft other designs within those categories without step-by-step instructions. However, it is still difficult to place many patterns in their proper categories and to see the underlying grid that makes drafting the pattern relatively easy. Therefore, in this book I have sorted the patterns into their proper categories first and then have presented a grid sheet as an aid in drafting the designs more easily. The use of the grid is explained at the end of this chapter.

BASIC CATEGORIES

The secret of successful pattern drafting is being able to look at a design and divide it visually into units. Most designs fit into a grid, which can be defined as the number of squares into which a pattern block is divided. In the case of eight-pointed star and hexagon designs, the grid is not composed of squares, but of diagonal lines radiating from the center of the unit. Once one has the proper grid for a design, drafting the pattern is simply a matter of connecting various grid lines with straight or diagonal lines. The ability to recognize the categories that patterns fall into not only makes it much easier to draft the designs, but also to identify patterns you may want to look up. Wherever possible, I have tried to group similar designs together. The basic categories used in this book and into which almost all patterns fall are given on the following pages.

FOUR-PATCH

The four-patch category is divided into three parts: designs in which the grid has four, sixteen, or sixty-four squares. Sometimes it is easiest to recognize a grid by counting the divisions across a block. For instance, a four square grid has two divisions; a sixteen square grid has four; and a sixty-four square grid has eight divisions across the block.

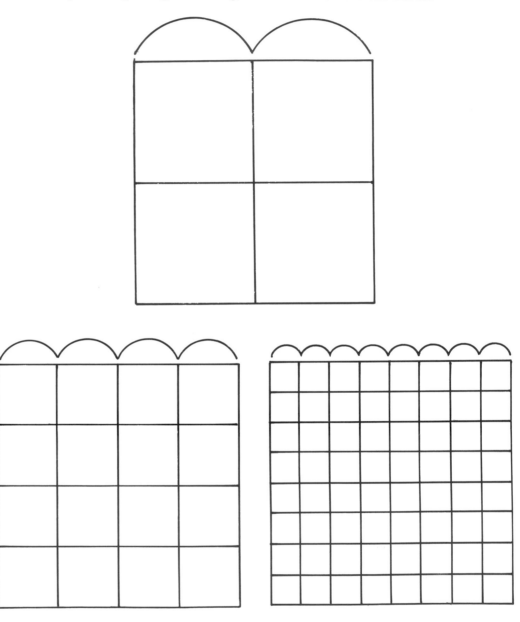

NINE-PATCH

The nine-patch category has two basic parts: designs with a grid of either nine or thiry-six squares, that is to say, ones with either three or six divisions across the block.

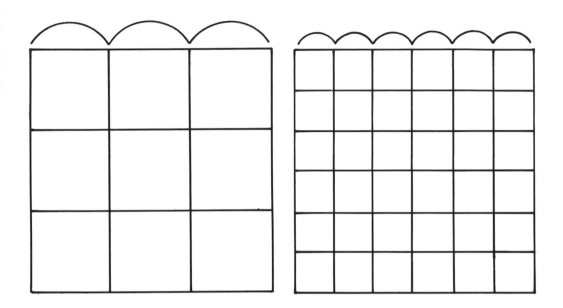

FIVE-PATCH

Five-patch designs are ones which require a grid of twenty-five squares and have five divisions across the block. Some patterns in this category require a one hundred square grid—one with ten divisions.

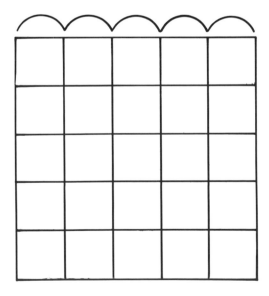

SEVEN-PATCH

Seven-patch designs are those requiring a grid of forty-nine squares and seven divisions across the block.

  In all the above categories, the squares must be *equal.*

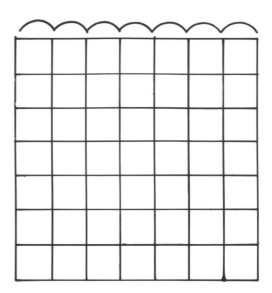

EIGHT-POINTED STAR

Eight-pointed star designs can be misleading. At first glance one might think these designs fall into the nine-patch category because there appear to be three divisions across the block. But in actual fact, the divisions are not *equal.* Eight-pointed star designs are *not* based on a grid of squares, but rather on a grid of equal divisions radiating from the center of the block.

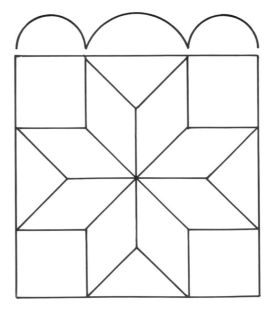

HEXAGON

Hexagon designs cannot fit within a square. They must be drafted by first making a hexagon and then dividing the hexagon to create various designs. Many hexagon designs are based on a six-pointed star drafted within the hexagon. There are two types of six-pointed stars: those with the points of the star going to the *sides* of the hexagon (#1), and those with the points going to the *corners* of the hexagon (#2).

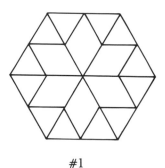

#1

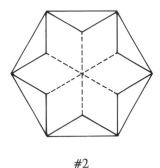

#2

CURVED DESIGNS

Most curved designs are actually based on one of the other categories, but have curved rather than straight lines connecting some of the lines of the grid. Other full circle curved designs such as the Sunburst are based on dividing the circle into a certain number of wedge-shaped units. Therefore, in categorizing the curved designs I have separated them into two groups: those which are based on various divisions of the circle—6, 8, 10 and so forth; and those which fall into one of the other categories such as 4 square four-patch, 16 square four-patch, 64 square four-patch, 9 square nine-patch. Any pattern containing a curve has been placed into the curved design category.

ISOLATED SQUARE DESIGNS

Some designs are made by first forming an isolated square in the center and then drafting the design outward from that. There are very few of these, however, since most of the patterns actually fit into one of the other categories.

PATTERNS WITH TWO OR MORE GRIDS

Sometimes a block will be divided into its basic units, then one portion of it will be further divided by using the grid of a *different* category. When this occurs, the block has been placed in its *basic* category according to how the square must be divided first in order to draft the design. Only a few of these patterns are shown; it is an area that is ripe for experimentation.

HOW TO USE THE GRIDS

All of the patterns in this book have been placed in categories according to their grids. However, even when the category to which a pattern belongs is known, it is sometimes hard to *see* the underlying grid and to be able to draft the pattern. Therefore, in the back of the book there is a transparent plastic sheet with the various grids printed on it. When you see a design that is difficult to draft, place the appropriate grid over the pattern and you will immediately see how to connect the lines of the grid with straight or curved lines to form the design.

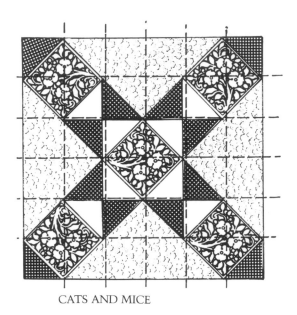

CATS AND MICE

The grids can also be used to make new designs. My last book explained how to create original designs by drafting two or more grids on the same piece of paper and then coloring in only certain lines to make new patterns. Using the grids provided in the back of this book, you can do the same thing. Since all the grids have been formed in the same size square, two or more may be placed on top of each other easily. When a piece of tracing paper is placed on top of this, it is possible to experiment by coloring in different portions of the lines until a design emerges that you like. Draft the same grids on whatever size square is needed and reproduce the design.

FOUR-PATCH DESIGNS

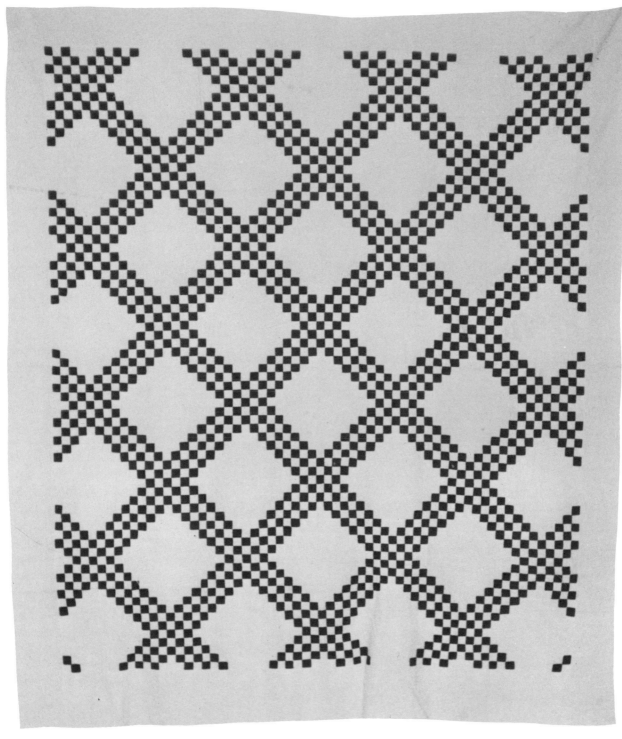

Irish Chain, antique quilt top, ca. 1850.

SECTION 1: FOUR SQUARE DESIGNS

Four-Patch
Broken Dishes

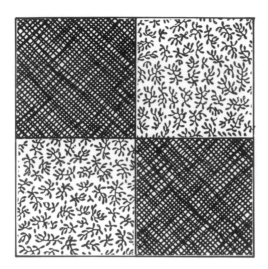
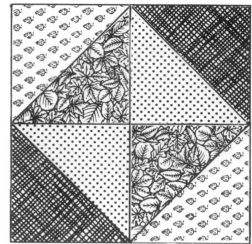

**Crow's Foot, Fan Mill,
Fly, Kathy's Ramble,
Sugar Bowl**
*Romance of the Patchwork
Quilt in America*, 1935

Yankee Puzzle

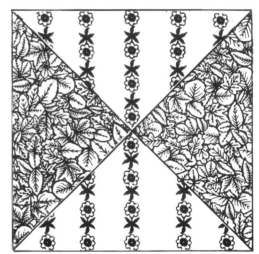

Turnstile, *Ladies' Art
Company,* 1928
**Churn Dash, Old Windmill,
Whirligig, Windmill**

Right and Left, *The Farm
and Fireside,* 1884,
Thrift Block

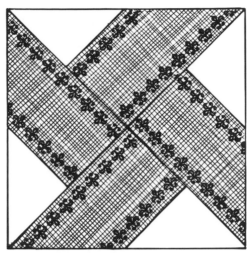

Four-Patch Designs

Big Dipper, *Ladies' Art Company,* 1898
Bow Ties, Yankee Puzzle

Twin Sisters, *Ladies' Art Company,* 1898
Churn Dash, Lone Star, Mill Wheel, Right and Left, Water Wheel, Whirlwind, Windmill

Washington's Puzzle, *Ladies' Art Company,* 1898
Checkerboard Skew, by Beth Gutcheon

SECTION 2: 16 SQUARE DESIGNS

Necktie, *Ladies' Art Company,* 1898
Bow Tie, Colonial Bow Tie, True Lover's Knot

Mosaic, No. 17, *Ladies' Art Company,* 1898
Ann and Andy

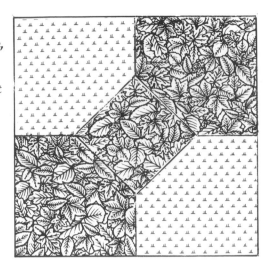 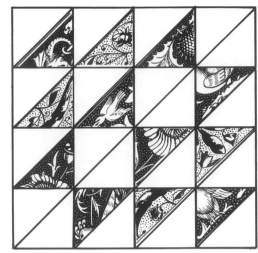

Road to Oklahoma, *Ladies' Art Company,* 1898
New Four-Patch

Mosaic No. 9, *Ladies' Art Company,* 1898
Milly's Favorite

Ladies' Wreath, *Ladies' Art Company,* 1898

The Anvil, *Old Patchwork Quilts,* 1929
Anvil

 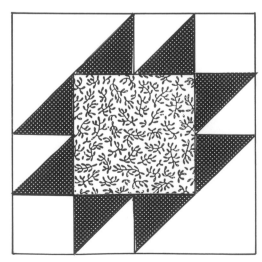

Four-Patch Designs

Double X, *Quilts, Their Story and How to Make Them,* 1915
The Swallow

Yankee Puzzle, *Ladies' Art Company,* 1898

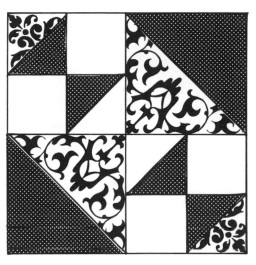

Old Maid's Puzzle, *Ladies' Art Company,* 1898
Double X, Hour Glass

Crosses and Losses, *Ladies' Art Company,* 1898
Fox and Geese

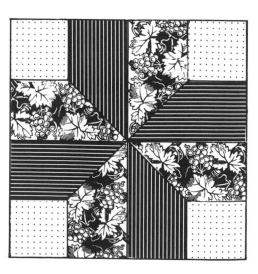

Double X, No. 3, *Ladies' Art Company,* 1898

Nelson's Victory, *Practical Needlework,* ca. 1910

Four-Patch Designs

Mr. Roosevelt's Necktie, *Practical Needlework,* ca. 1910
Oh Susannah, Susannah Patch

Windmill, *Ladies' Art Company,* 1898

Contrary Husband, *Kansas City Star,* 1938
Box Car Patch, Churn Dash

Churn Dash, *Ladies' Art Company,* 1898

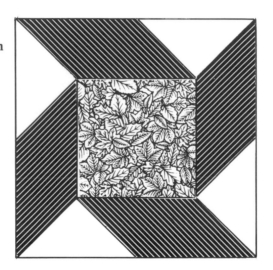

Art Square, *Ladies' Art Company,* 1898
Village Square

Mosaic, No. 1, *Ladies' Art Company,* 1898

Four-Patch Designs

Mosaic, No. 21, *Ladies' Art Company,* 1898

Ring Around the Posey, by Marcia Aasmundstad, 1980

Mosaic, No. 5, *Ladies' Art Company,* 1898

Mosaic, No. 2, *Ladies' Art Company,* 1898

Triangle Squares, *Virginia Snow Patchwork Designs,* ca. 1930

Economy, *Ladies' Art Company,* 1898

41

Four-Patch Designs

The Blockade, *Kansas City Star,* 1938

Windblown Square, *101 Patchwork Patterns,* 1931
Balkan Puzzle, Windblown Star

Mosaic, No. 6, *Ladies' Art Company,* 1898

Mosaic, No. 16, *Ladies' Art Company,* 1898
Connecticut

Mosaic, No. 22, *Ladies' Art Company,* 1898

New England Star, by Holice Turnbow, 1979

Four-Patch Designs

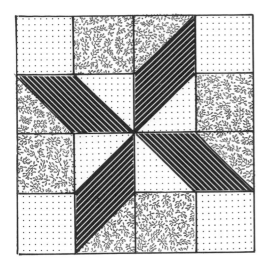

Shooting Star, *Ladies' Art Company,* 1898
Clay's Choice, Clay's Favorite, Harry's Star, Henry of the West, Stardust Quilt, Star of the West

Mosaic, No. 18, *Ladies' Art Company,* 1898
Old Poinsettia Block, Spinning Stars

Wheels

Chevron

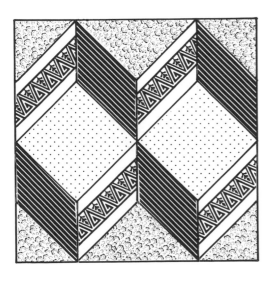

Patience Corners, *Ladies' Art Company,* 1898

Dutchman's Puzzle, *Ladies' Art Company,* 1898
Mosaic

43

Four-Patch Designs

Windmill, *Practical
Needlework,* ca. 1910
**Devil's Dark House,
Devil's Puzzle, Fly Foot,
Swastika, Winding Blades**

Star of Beauty, *Practical
Needlework,* ca. 1910
**July Fourth, Next Door
Neighbor, Patriotic Quilt,
Star of Beauty**

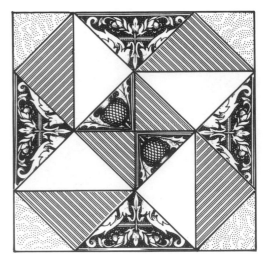

Bachelor's Puzzle, *Romance
of the Patchwork Quilt in
America,* 1935

Godey Design, *Godey's
Lady's Book,* 1857
Mosaic, No. 3

A Snowflake, *Ladies' Art
Company,* 1898
Cross Stitch, Snow Block

The House Jack Built,
Ladies' Art Company,
1898
Triple Stripe

Four-Patch Designs

Old Tippecanoe, *Ladies' Art Company,* 1898
Wheel of Time

Sawtooth, *The Farm and Fireside,* 1884
A Smaller Star, Cluster of Stars, Evening Star, Nameless Star

Ribbon Star, *Ladies' Art Company,* 1898
Crystal Star, Evening Star

Mosaic, No. 19, *Ladies' Art Company,* 1898

Mosaic, No. 15, *Ladies' Art Company,* 1898

Mosaic, No. 10, *Ladies' Art Company,* 1898

45

Four-Patch Designs

Centennial, *Ladies' Art Company,* 1898

Missouri Star, *Quilting,* 1934

Indian Star, *Kansas City Star,* 1937

Diamond Star, *Practical Needlework,* ca. 1910
Barbara Fritchie Star, Pieced Star

A Unique Design, *Ladies' Home Journal,* 1896
Mosaic, No. 13, Pieced Star, Star Puzzle

Double Z, *Ladies' Art Company,* 1898
Brown Goose, Gray Goose, Old Maid's Puzzle #2

Four-Patch Designs

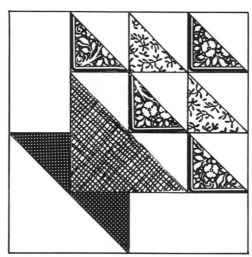

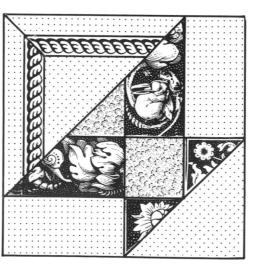

Whirligig I, by Marcia
Aasmundstad, 1980

Whirligig II, by Marcia
Aasmundstad, 1980

Mosaic, No. 11, *Ladies'
Art Company,* 1898

Flower Basket, *Ladies' Art
Company,* 1898

Basket Quilt, *Ladies' Art
Company,* 1898

Dresden Basket, *Virginia
Snow Patchwork Designs*
ca. 1930

Four-Patch Designs

The Disk, *Ladies' Art Company,* 1898

Some Pretty Patchwork, date unknown

 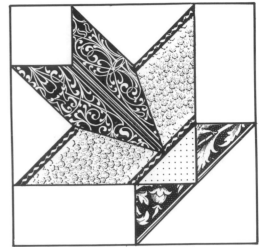

Virginia Star, by Hazel Carter, 1976

Christmas Star, by Hazel Carter, 1976

 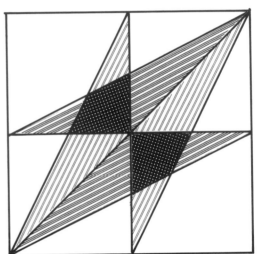

Concorde Star, by Hazel Carter, first published in *The Quilter's Newsletter* magazine, November 1976

Texas Tears, *Ladies' Art Company,* 1898

48

Star and Cross, *Ladies' Art Company,* 1898

SECTION 3: 64 SQUARE DESIGNS

New Four-Patch, *The Farm and Fireside,* 1884, **Jacob's Ladder, World's Fair Block**

Milky Way, *Ladies's Art Company,* 1928 **Indiana Puzzle**

Sunshine, *Ladies' Art Company,* 1898

Blindman's Fancy, *Ladies' Art Company,* 1898

Four-Patch Designs

Barrister's Block, *Ladies'*
Art Company, 1898

Kansas Troubles, *Ladies'*
Art Company, 1898

Irish Puzzle, Bear's Paw,
Ladies' Art Company, 1898
Climbing Rose, Flying
Dutchman, Forest Path,
Indian Trail, Indian Trails,
Kansas Troubles, North
Wind, Old Maid's Ramble,
Prickly Pear, Rambling
Road, Rambling Rose,
Storm at Sea, Tangled
Tares, Weather Vane,
Winding Walk

World's Fair Puzzle,
Ladies' Art Company, 1898

Navajo, *Ladies' Art*
Company, 1928
Indian Mats

Evergreen Tree, *Virginia*
Snow Patchwork Designs,
ca. 1930

50

Palm Leaf, *Ladies' Art Company,* 1922 **Hosanna**

Secret Drawer, *Kansas City Star,* 1930

Ring of Fortune, by Marcia Aasmundstad, 1980

Double T, *101 Patchwork Patterns,* 1931 **Eight-Pointed Star**

Sarah's Favorite, *Ladies' Art Company,* 1898

Toad-in-the-Puddle, *Ladies' Art Company,* 1898 **Rambler**

Four-Patch Designs

Railroad Crossing, *Ladies' Art Company,* 1898

Jacob's Ladder, *Virginia Snow Patchwork Designs,* ca. 1930

Old Maid's Ramble, *Ladies' Art Company,* 1898
Crimson Rambler, Spring Beauty, Vermont

Snail Trail, *Ladies' Art Company,* 1928
Indiana Puzzle, Virginia Reel, Whirligig

Double Squares, *Ladies' Art Company,* 1898

Mosaic, No. 7, *Ladies' Art Company,* 1898
Jack-in-the-Pulpit, Toad in the Puddle

Pinwheel Square, by
Marcia Aasmundstad, 1980

Godey Design, *Godey's
Lady's Book,* 1851

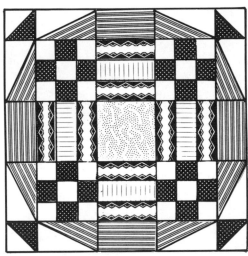

Fanny's Favorite, *Ladies'
Art Company,* 1928

Spider's Den, *Ladies' Art
Company,* 1898

Squares and Stripes,
Ladies' Art Company, 1898
Triangles and Stripes

Home Treasure, *Ladies'
Art Company,* 1898

Four-Patch Designs

Storm at Sea, *Ladies' Art Company,* 1898
Rolling Stone

Springfield Patch, *Ladies' Art Company,* 1928

1904 Star, *Practical Needlework,* ca. 1910

Annapolis Patch, *Ladies' Art Company,* 1898

Stars and Squares, *Ladies' Art Company,* 1898
Rising Star, Rising Star and Square

Eight Hands Around, *Ladies' Art Company,* 1898

Four-Patch Designs

Odd Fellow's Chain, *Ladies' Art Company,* 1898
San Diego

Crow's Foot, *Ladies' Art Company,* 1898
Arrowheads, Crow Foot

Blackford's Beauty, *Ladies' Art Company,* 1898
Arrowheads, Black Beauty, Good Cheer, Star and Stripe, Stepping Stones

Missouri Puzzle, *Ladies' Art Company,* 1928

Mother's Fancy, *Ladies' Art Company,* 1898

Lena's Choice, *Practical Needlework,* ca. 1910

Four-Patch Designs

Old Spanish Tile, *Kansas City Star,* 1933

Devil's Claws, *Ladies' Art Company,* 1898,
Bright Stars, Cross Plains, Idaho Beauty, Lily, Sweet Gum Leaf

The Feathered Edge Star, *101 Patchwork Patterns,* 1931

Baton Rouge Block, *Ladies' Art Company,* 1928

Johnnie Around the Corner, *Ladies' Art Company,* 1898
Broken Wheel

Tulip Lady Finger *Ladies' Art Company,* 1898

Four-Patch Designs

Ocean Waves, *The Romance of the Patchwork Quilt In America,* 1935

Coxey's Camp, *Ladies' Art Company,* 1898
Coxey's Army

Odds and Ends, *Ladies' Art Company,* 1898

Flower Pot, *Grandmother Clark's Authentic Early American Quilts,* 1932

Square and Star, *Ladies' Art Company,* 1898

Seattle Sights, by Alice Newton, 1979

57

Four-Patch Designs

World's Fair, *Virginia Snow Patchwork Designs,* ca. 1930

Michigan Beauty, *Practical Needlework,* ca. 1910
Fairlington Square, by Marilyn Gould
Idaho, Many Pointed Star

The V Block, *Ladies' Art Company,* 1922

Advisor's Block, by Hazel Carter, 1973

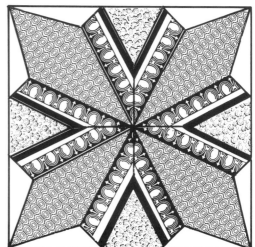

Devil's Puzzle, *Ladies' Art Company,* 1898
Fly-Foot

Rockets, by Judy Spahn, 1979

Four-Patch Designs

Iowa Star Block, *Ladies' Art Company,* 1928

Key West Beauty, *Ladies' Art Company,* 1928

Dervish Star, *Virginia Snow Patchwork Designs,* ca. 1930

Dutch Windmill, *Ladies' Art Company,* 1898

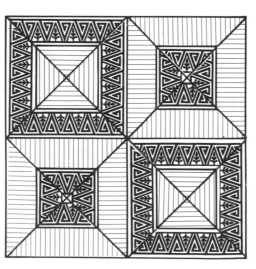

Cross within a Cross, *Ladies' Art Company,* 1898

Mosaic, No. 4, *Ladies' Art Company,* 1898

Four-Patch Designs

Grandmother's Own, *Ladies' Art Company,* 1898
Four Square,
Grandmother's Dream

T Quilt, *Ladies' Art Company,* 1898

Magic Circle, *Ladies' Art Company,* 1898

Crazy Ann, *Ladies' Art Company,* 1898
Firewheel, Pinwheel,
Swastika

Chimney Sweep, *Old Patchwork Quilts,* 1929
Album, Album Patch,
Friendship Chain,
Courthouse Square

Roman Cross, Washington Sidewalk, *Ladies' Art Company,* 1898
Chicago Pavements

Kentucky Chain, *Practical Needlework,* ca. 1910

Dove in the Window, *Kansas City Star,* 1932

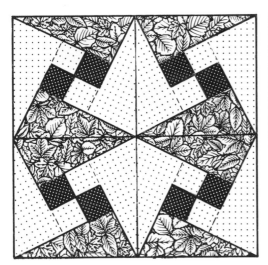

Arabic Lattice, *Ladies' Art Company,* 1898

Honeycomb, *Ladies' Art Company,* 1898

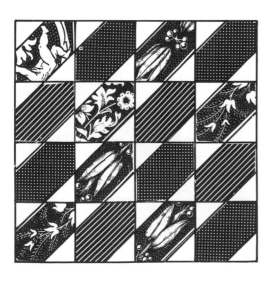

The Xquisite, *Ladies' Art Company,* 1898

Cube Lattice, *Ladies' Art Company,* 1898
Idle Moments

Four-Patch Designs

Godey Design, *Godey's Lady's Book,* 1851
Twist Patchwork, Plaited Block, Ribbon Twist

Godey Design, *Godey's Lady's Book,* 1851
Five Cross, Kansas Dugout, Lovely Patchwork

Tallahassee Quilt Block, *Ladies' Art Company,* 1928

NINE-PATCH DESIGNS

California Sunset, wall hanging, by Jinny Beyer.

SECTION 1: NINE SQUARE DESIGNS

Shoo-fly, *Ladies' Art Company,* 1898

Double X, No. 1, *Ladies' Art Company,* 1898
Tennessee, Three and Six

 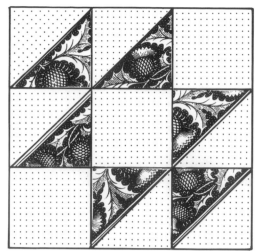

Split Nine-Patch, *The Romance of the Patchwork Quilt in America,* 1935

Fred's Spool, *Practical Needlework,* ca. 1910
Empty Spools, Spool

 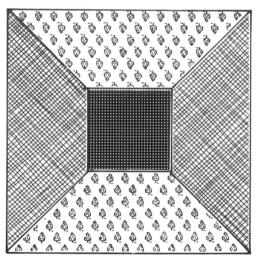

Aunt Eliza's Star Quilt, *Ladies' Art Company,* 1898
Aunt Lottie's Star

Godey Design, *Godey's Lady's Book,* 1862
Mosaic Patchwork, Eight Point Design, Flying Crows, Happy Home, Lone Star, Ohio Star, Texas Star, Variable Star

Nine-Patch Designs

Godey Design, *Godey's Lady's Book,* 1858
Swamp Patch

Frank Leslie Design, *Frank Leslie's Modenwelt,* 1871
Silent Star, Star X

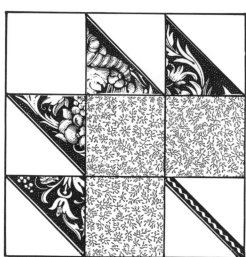

The Practical Orchard, *Ladies' Art Company,* 1898
Hour Glass #2

Maple Leaf, Magnolia Leaf, *Practical Needlework,* ca. 1910
Apple Leaf, Tea Leaves

Box Quilt Pattern, *Ladies' Art Company,* 1898

Boy's Nonsense, *Ladies' Art Company,* 1898
Nonsense

SECTION 2: 36 SQUARE DESIGNS

Cactus Flower, *The Romance of the Patchwork Quilt in America,* 1935

Texas Flower, *Ladies' Art Company,* 1898
Cactus Flower

Basket of Scraps

The Railroad, *Ladies' Art Company,* 1898
Blue Chains, Golden Stairs, Jacob's Ladder, Stepping Stones, Tail of Benjamin Franklin's Kite, The Trail of the Covered Wagon, Underground Railroad, Wagon Tracks, Western Reserve

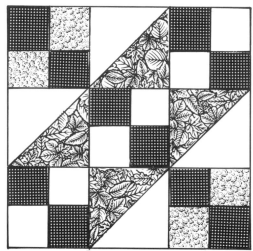

Dublin Steps, *Virginia Snow Patchwork Designs,* ca. 1930

Hayes Corner, designed in 1972 for Dottie Hayes, by Beth Gutcheon. First published in *The Perfect Patchwork Primer,* 1973

The Cat's Cradle, *Kansas City Star,* 1934

Rolling Stone, *Ladies' Art Company,* 1898
Block Circle, Broken Wheel, Johnnie Round the Corner, Peek-a-boo

Grecian Designs, *Ladies' Art Company,* 1898
Broken Plate, Churn Dash, Double Monkey Wrench, Greek Cross, Greek Square, Hole-in-the-barn-door, Lincoln's Platform, Love Knot, Puss-in-the-corner, Sherman's March, Shoo-fly

Flutter Wheel, *Ladies' Art Company,* 1898
Pin Wheels

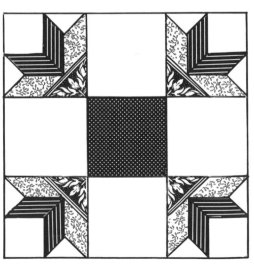

Modern Tulip, *Virginia Snow Patchwork Designs,* ca. 1930

Sage Bud, *Kansas City Star,* 1930
Turkey Tracks

Nine-Patch Designs

W.C.T. Union, *Ladies' Art Company,* 1898

Tassal Plant, *Ladies' Art Company,* 1898

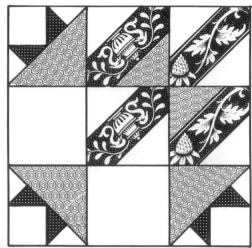

Nonsuch, *Ladies' Art Company,* 1898

Indian Hatchet, *Ladies' Art Company,* 1898

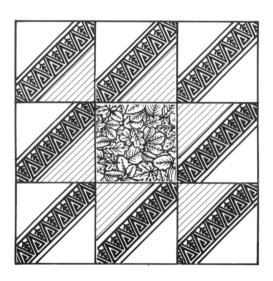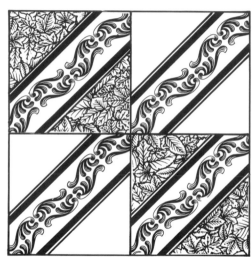

Little Rock Block, *Ladies' Art Company,* 1928
Arkansas Star, Butterfly Block, Star of the Sea

Star A, *Ladies' Art Company,* 1898
An "A" Star

Sawtooth Patchwork, *Ladies' Art Company,* 1898

Combination Star, *Ladies' Art Company,* 1898

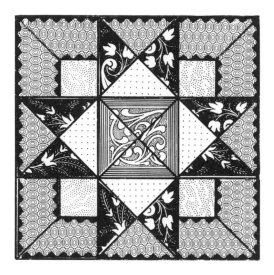

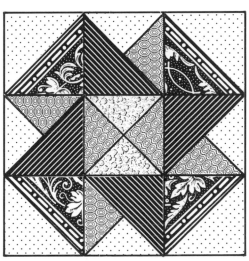

Four Corners, *Virginia Snow Patchwork Designs,* ca. 1930

Card Trick, by Jeffrey Gutcheon, first published in *The Perfect Patchwork Primer,* 1973

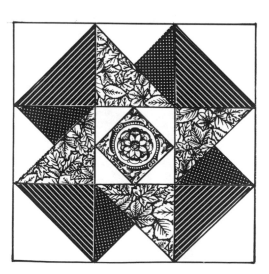

Air Castle, *Ladies' Art Company,* 1898
Towers of Camelot

Star of Hope, by Marcia Aasmundstad, 1980

Nine-Patch Designs

Dolly Madison Star, *The Romance of the Patchwork Quilt in America,* 1935
President's Block

Santa Fe Block, *Ladies' Art Company,* 1928

Grandma's Star, *Practical Needlework,* ca. 1910
Blue Meteors, 54-40 or Fight, The Railroad Quilt

Judy in Arabia, by Jeffrey Gutcheon, first published in *The Quilt Design Workbook,* 1976

Storm at Sea

California Sunset, by Jinny Beyer, designed for the Patch In Time Quilt Conference, San Francisco, 1979

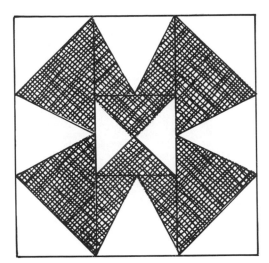

Nine-Patch Designs

Double Z, *Ladies' Art Company,* 1898

Hand Weave, *Ladies' Art Company,* 1928

Morning Star, *Ladies' Art Company,* 1898
Bright Star

Mosaic, No. 8, *Ladies' Art Company,* 1898

Five Patch, *Ladies' Art Company,* 1898
New Nine-Patch

London Roads, *Ladies' Art Company,* 1898
Broken Dish, Fireside, Visitor

Nine-Patch Designs

Tangled Garter, *Ladies'*
Art Company, 1898
Garden Maze, Queen of
May, Sun Dial, Tirza's
Treasure

Beggar Blocks, *Ladies' Art*
Company, 1898
Cats and Mice, Spool and
Bobbin

Arkansas Traveler, *Ladies'*
Art Company, 1898

Joseph's Coat, Nancy
Cabot Newspaper Column,
ca. 1930

Mollie's Choice, *Ladies'*
Art Company, 1898

Columbian Star, *Ladies'*
Art Company, 1898

Nine-Patch Designs

Hour Glass, *Ladies' Art Company,* 1898

Country Farm, *Ladies' Art Company,* 1898

Gentleman's Fancy

Pointed Star, by Marcia Aasmundstad, 1980

Capital T, *Ladies' Art Company,* 1898

Double T, *Kansas City Star,* 1937

73

Nine-Patch Designs

Swing in the Center
Ladies' Art Company, 1898
**Mrs. Roosevelt's Favorite,
Roman Pavement**

Merry Kite, *Ladies' Art
Company,* 1928

Union, *Ladies' Art
Company,* 1898
Four Crowns

Robbing Peter to Pay Paul,
Ladies' Art Company, 1898
Arizona

Mixed T, *Ladies' Art
Company,* 1898

T Quartette, *Ladies' Art
Company,* 1898

 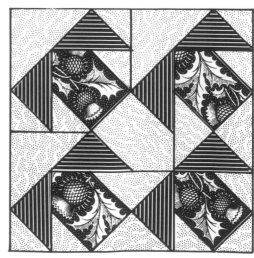

Godey Design, *Godey's Lady's Book,* 1858

Braced Star, *Ladies' Art Company,* 1928

Album Blocks, *Ladies' Art Company,* 1898
Tricolor Star

Boxes, Nancy Page Pattern, ca. 1930

Northumberland Star, *Practical Needlework,* ca. 1910

Chicago Star, *Ladies' Art Company,* 1898

Nine-Patch Designs

Miss Jackson, *Ladies' Art Company,* 1922
Empty Spools, Prosperity Block

Robin's Nest, by Robin Ellen Kuhn, 1979

Chain

Sky Rocket

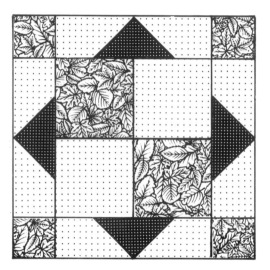 

Sky Rocket, *101 Patchwork Patterns,* 1931
The Album, Dogtooth Violet

Royal Star Quilt, *Ladies' Art Company,* 1922

Nine-Patch Designs

A Beauty, *Practical Needlework,* ca. 1910

Mrs. Bryan's Choice, *Practical Needlework,* ca. 1910

Corn and Beans, *Ladies' Art Company,* 1898
Duck and Ducklings, Handy Andy, Hen and Chicks, Shoo-fly

Memory, *Practical Needlework,* ca. 1910

Rippling Star, by Marcia Aasmundstad, 1980

Best of All, *Practical Needlework,* ca. 1910

Nine-Patch Designs

Star Light, by Marcia
Aasmundstad, 1980

Union Star, *Practical
Needlework,* ca. 1910

Pinwheel and Squares, by
Marcia Aasmundstad, 1980

Aunt Sukey's Choice, *The
Romance of the Patchwork
Quilt in America,* 1935
**Puss-in-Boots, Puss-in-the-
corner**

Weather Vane, *101 Patchwork Patterns,* 1931

Rosebud, *Ladies' Art
Company,* 1898
**Bright Star,
Hummingbird**

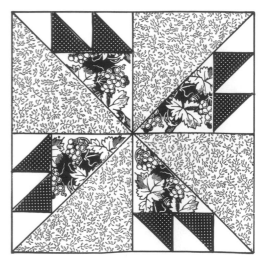

Pine Tree

Lost Ship Pattern, *Ladies' Art Company,* 1898

Cut Glass Dish, *Ladies' Art Company,* 1898
Winged Square

Mrs. Cleveland's Choice, *Ladies' Art Company,* 1898
County Fair, Square within Square

Swastika Patch, *Ladies' Art Company,* 1928

Rolling Pin Wheel, *Ladies' Art Company,* 1898
Pin Wheel Star, Whirling Pin Wheel

Nine-Patch Designs

Flying Dutchman, *Ladies' Art Company,* 1898

Spools, *Ladies' Art Company,* 1898

Rumpelstiltskin's Frolic, by Kathryn Kuhn, 1978

Double X, No. 4, *Ladies' Art Company,* 1898

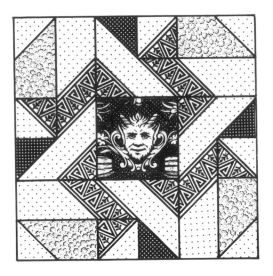

Flagstones, Snowball, *Ladies' Art Company,* 1928
Four and Nine Patch, Tile Puzzle

Domino, *Ladies' Art Company,* 1898

Nine-Patch Designs

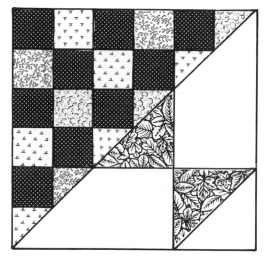
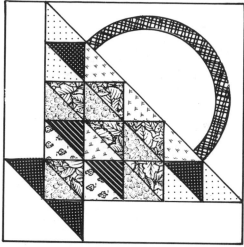

Steps to the Altar, *Ladies' Art Company,* 1898
Fruit Dish

Cherry Basket, *Ladies' Art Company,* 1898
Pieced Basket

Golgotha, *Old Patchwork Quilts,* 1929
Cross upon Cross, The Three Crosses

Wild Goose Chase, *101 Patchwork Patterns,* 1931

Cats and Mice, *Ladies' Art Company,* 1898

Building Blocks, *Virginia Snow Patchwork Designs,* ca. 1930
Jerusalem Road, Pin Wheel Road to Jerusalem

Nine-Patch Designs

St. Louis Star, *Practical Needlework,* ca. 1910

Quilt Block, *Ladies' Art Company,* 1898
Four Points

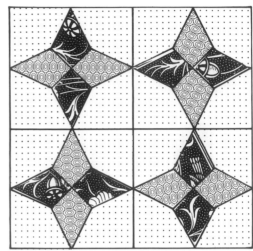

Vice President's Quilt, *Ladies' Art Company,* 1898

Nine-Patch Kaleidoscope, by Jinny Beyer, 1977

Morning Patch, *Ladies' Art Company,* 1922

The Mayflower, *Ladies' Art Company,* 1898

Nine-Patch Designs

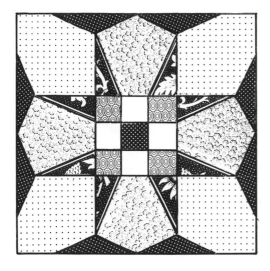

Klondike Star, *Practical Needlework, ca. 1910*

St. Louis Star, *The Romance of the Patchwork Quilt in America, 1935*

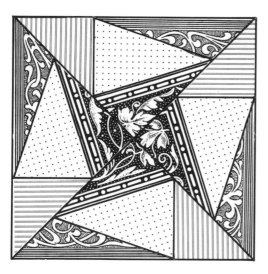

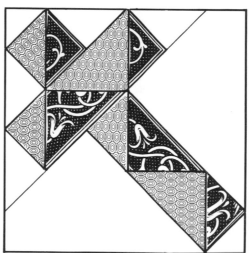

Entertaining Motions, by Beth Gutcheon, 1980

The Cross, *Ladies' Art Company, 1898*

The World's Fair, *Ladies' Art Company, 1898*

Turkey Tracks, *Ladies' Art Company, 1898*
Resolutions

Nine-Patch Designs

Pine Tree, *Ladies' Art Company,* 1898

Virginia Reel, *Practical Needlework,* ca. 1910
Tangled Lines

Four Points, *Ladies' Art Company,* 1898
Fort Sumter

Charm, *Ladies' Art Company,* 1898 This block requires both a four- and nine-patch grid.

FIVE-PATCH DESIGNS

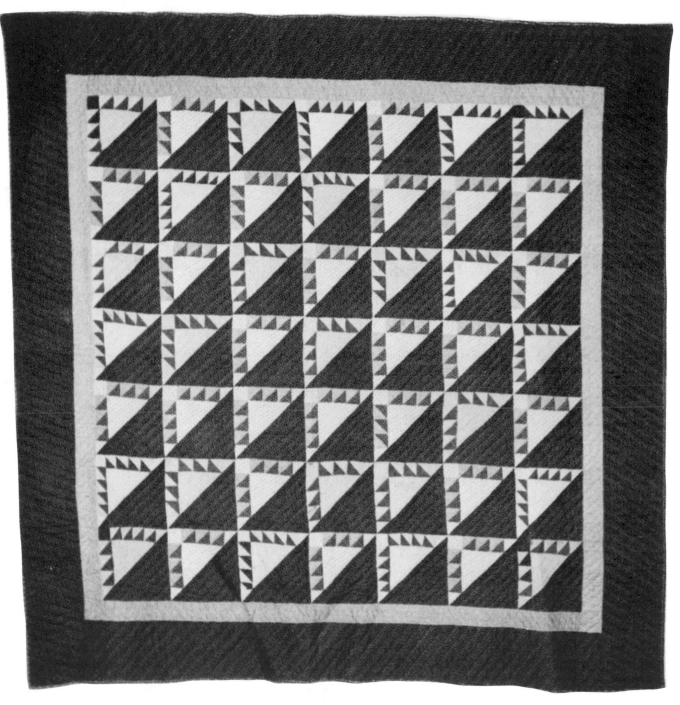

Lady of the Lake, antique quilt of calico, ca. 1880.

Five-Patch Designs

Puss in the Corner, *Ladies' Art Company,* 1898
Kitten in the Corner, Kitty Corner, Tic-Tac-Toe

Children's Delight, *Ladies' Art Company,* 1898

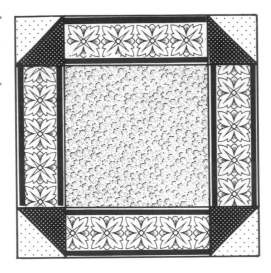

King's Crown, *Ladies' Art Company,* 1898
John's Favorite

Clown, *Ladies' Art Company,* 1928

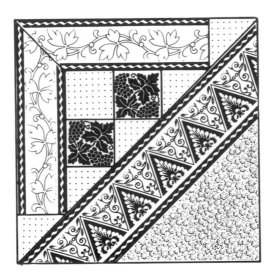

Crazy House, *Ladies Art Company,* 1928

Lady of the Lake, *Ladies' Art Company,* 1898

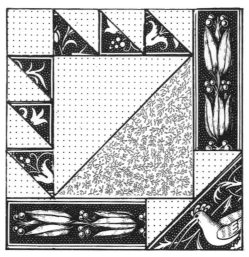

Star of Hope, *Ladies' Art Company,* 1928

Cake Stand, *Ladies' Art Company,* 1898

May Basket, *Farmer's Wife Book of Quilts,* 1931
Fruit Basket

Grape Basket, *Ladies' Art Company,* 1898

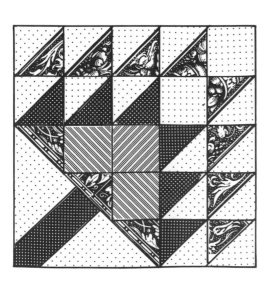

Pine Tree, *Grandmother Clark's Authentic Early American Quilts,* 1932

Tree of Paradise, *Quilts, Their Story and How to Make Them,* 1915
Pine Tree

Five-Patch Designs

Sky Rocket, *Virginia Snow Patchwork Designs,* ca. 1930

Double Wrench, *Ladies' Art Company,* 1898
Chinese Coin, French Fours, Pioneer Block

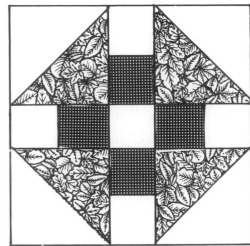

Handy Andy, *Ladies' Art Company,* 1898
Foot Stool

Square and a Half, *Ladies' Art Company,* 1898

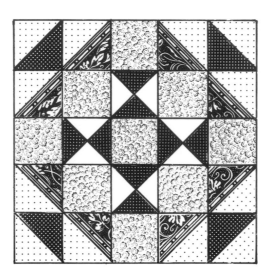

Wedding Ring, *Ladies' Art Company,* 1898
Mill Wheel, Nest and Fledgling, Single Wedding Ring

Pigeon Toes, by Beth Gutcheon, first published in *The Perfect Patchwork Primer,* 1973

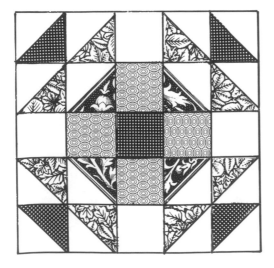

Five-Patch Designs

Farmer's Daughter, *Ladies' Art Company,* 1898
Corner Posts, Flying Birds, Miller's Daughter, Rolling Star

Four X Star, *Ladies' Art Company,* 1898

Providence Quilt Block, *Ladies' Art Company,* 1898

Sister's Choice, *Ladies' Art Company,* 1898
Fool's Square

Grandmother's Cross, *101 Patchwork Patterns,* 1931

King David's Crown, *The Romance of the Patchwork Quilt in America,* 1935

Five-Patch Designs

Memory Block, *The Romance of the Patchwork Quilt in America,* 1935

Star I, by Marcia Aasmundstad, 1980

Star II, by Marcia Aasmundstad, 1980

Triangle Puzzle, *Virginia Snow Patchwork Designs,* ca. 1930

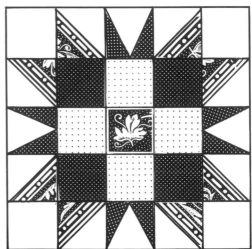

St. Louis Star, *Ladies' Art Company,* 1898

Garden of Eden, *Ladies' Art Company,* 1898
Economy

Red Cross, *Ladies' Art Company,* 1898

Bachelor's Puzzle, *Ladies' Art Company,* 1898

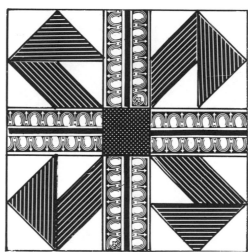

Duck and Ducklings, *Ladies' Art Company,* 1898
Corn and Beans, Fox and Geese, Grandmother's Choice, Handy Andy, Hen and Chickens, Shoo-fly, Wild Goose Chase

Jack in the Box, *101 Patchwork Patterns,* 1931
Wheel of Fortune

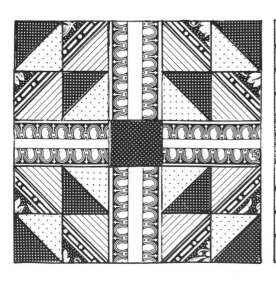

Handy Andy, *The Romance of the Patchwork Quilt in America,* 1935
Flying Geese

Premium Star, *Ladies' Art Company,* 1898

Five-Patch Designs

Odd Star, *Ladies' Art Company,* 1898

Uncle Sam's Favorite, *Practical Needlework,* ca. 1910

Cross and Crown, *Ladies' Art Company,* 1898
Bouquets, Goose Tracks

Cross and Crown, *The Romance of the Patchwork Quilt in America,* 1935
Mexican Star, Point and Feather

 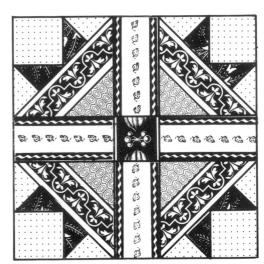

Goose Tracks

Fanny's Fan, *Ladies' Art Company,* 1898

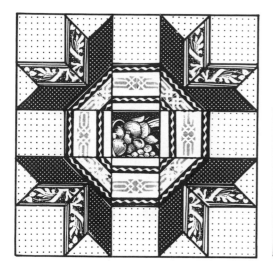

David and Goliath,
Quilting, 1934
**Bull's Eye, Doe and Darts,
Flying Darts, Four Darts**

Ladies' Delight, *Ladies'
Art Company,* 1898

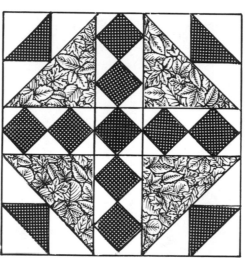

Pin Wheel Square, *Ladies'
Art Company,* 1898
Follow the Leader

Bird's Nest, *Ladies' Art
Company,* 1898

Joseph's Coat, *Ladies' Art
Company,* 1898
Lewis and Clark

Rocky Glen, *Ladies' Art
Company,* 1898

Five-Patch Designs

Album, *Ladies' Art Company,* 1898

Domino and Square, *Ladies' Art Company,* 1898

Godey Design, *Godey's Lady's Book,* 1851

An Effective Square, *Ladies' Home Journal,* 1896
Odd Fellows, Odd Fellow's Patch

Godey Design, *Godey's Lady's Book,* 1858

Simple Design, *Ladies' Art Company,* 1898

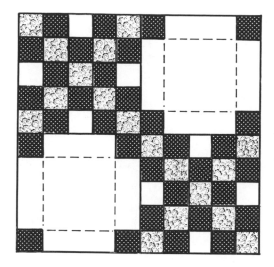

Double Irish Chain, *Ladies' Art Company,* 1898

Linton, *Ladies' Art Company,* 1898

All Kinds, *Ladies' Art Company,* 1898

My Star, by Lesly-Claire Greenberg, 1978

Friendship, *Kansas City Star,* 1938

Checkered Star, by Marcia Aasmundstad, 1980

Five-Patch Designs

Star Lane, *Ladies' Art Company,* 1898

Four Z Patch, *Ladies' Art Company,* 1898

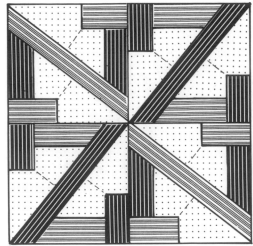

Tall Pine Tree, *The Romance of the Patchwork Quilt in America,* 1935

Queen Charlotte's Crown, Indian Meadow, *The Romance of the Patchwork Quilt in America,* 1935
Basket Design, Queen's Crown

Uncle Sam's Hourglass, *Practical Needlework,* ca. 1910

Cynthia Ann Dancing, by Beth Gutcheon, first published in *The Quilt Design Workbook,* 1976

Five-Patch Designs

Here is the Steeple, by Beth Gutcheon, first published in *The Quilt Design Workbook,* 1976

Star Wedge, *Virginia Snow Patchwork Designs,* ca. 1930

Poinsettia, by Fay Goldey, 1979

Album Quilt, *Ladies' Art Company,* 1898

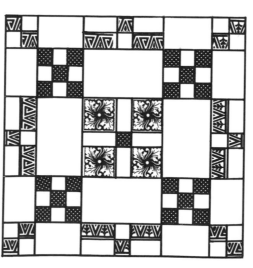

Goose in the Pond, *Ladies' Art Company,* 1898
Young Man's Fancy

Burgoyne's Quilt, *101 Patchwork Patterns,* 1931

SEVEN-PATCH DESIGNS

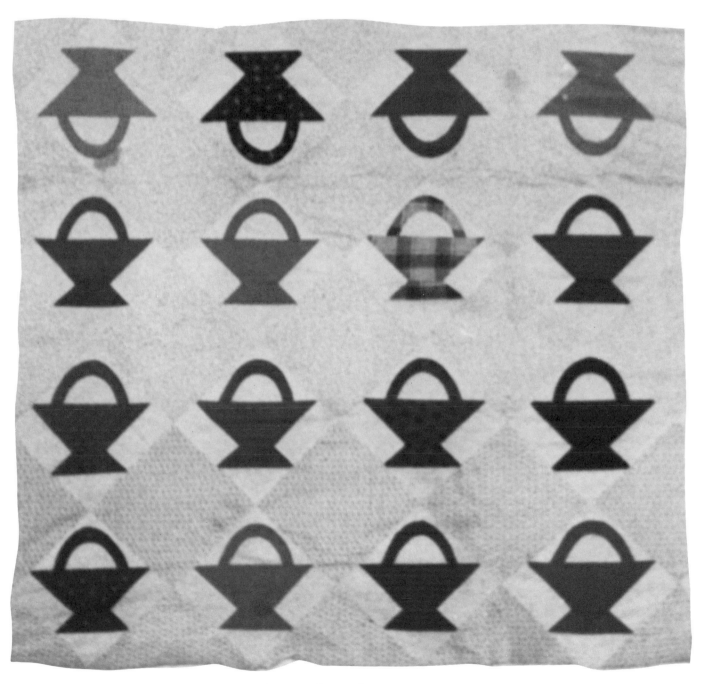

Flower Basket, quilt top, ca. 1920.

Seven-Patch Designs

Nine-Patch, *The Romance of The Patchwork Quilt in America,* 1935
Checkers

Lincoln's Platform, *Ladies' Art Company,* 1898

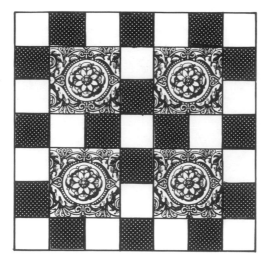

Greek Cross, *Practical Needlework,* ca. 1910

Prickly Pear, *The Romance of the Patchwork Quilt in America,* 1935

Hen and Chickens, *Ladies' Art Company,* 1898

Dove in the Window, *Ladies' Art Company,* 1898

100

Seven-Patch Designs

Bear's Foot, *Ladies' Art Company,* 1898
Bear's Paw, Duck's Foot, Duck's Foot-in-the-Mud, Hand of Friendship

Bear's Paw, The Best Friend, *Grandmother Clark's Authentic Early American Quilts,* 1932

Autumn Leaves, *Quilting,* 1934
Autumn Leaf, Maple Leaf, Peony

Stone Mason's Puzzle, *Ladies' Art Company,* 1922

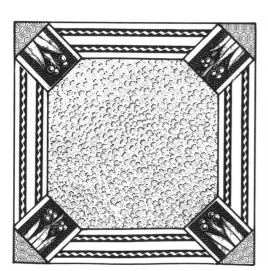

Mosaic Patchwork, *Dictionary of Needlework,* 1882
Tile Patchwork

Girl's Joy, *Ladies' Art Company,* 1898

Seven-Patch Designs

Persian, *Ladies' Art Company,* 1928

Our Country, *Kansas City Star,* 1939

T-Square #1, by Holice Turnbow, 1980

T-Square #2, by Holice Turnbow, 1980

Tree of Paradise, *The Romance of the Patchwork Quilt in America,* 1935

Feather Star, *Quilts, Their Story and How to Make Them,* 1915

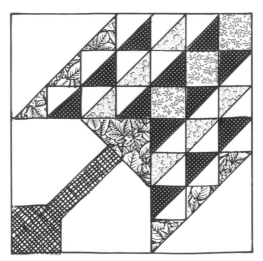 

EIGHT-POINTED STAR DESIGNS

Melon Patch, Amish quilt of wool, ca. 1920. Photograph by Steve Thompson.

Eight-Pointed Star Designs

Octagon, *Ladies' Art Company,* 1898
The Four Leaf Clover, Job's Troubles, Marble Floor, Melon Patch

Diamond and Star, *Ladies' Art Company,* 1898
Amethyst, Kaleidoscope, Kaleidoscopic Patch, Windmill Star

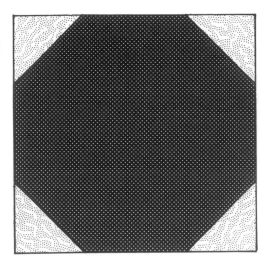
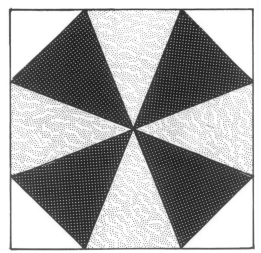

Godey Design, *Godey's Lady's Book,* 1852
Merry Go Round, Spider's Web

Propeller, by Jinny Beyer, 1978

Spider Web, variation

Gold Imari Block, by Lesly-Claire Greenberg, 1980

Eight-Pointed Star Designs

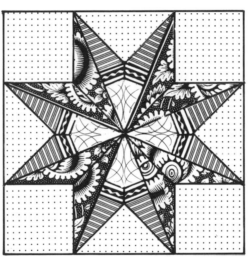

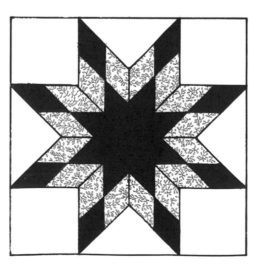

Eight-Pointed Star, *Ladies' Home Journal,* 1896
Star of Le-Moyne

Silver and Gold, Star of the East, *The Romance of the Patchwork Quilt in America,* 1935

V-Block

Kaleidostar, by Virginia Tolson, 1979

St. Louis Star, *The Romance of the Patchwork Quilt in America,* 1935

Unknown Star, Pierced Eight-Pointed Star, *Quilting,* 1934
Star upon Stars, Virginia Star

Eight-Pointed Star Designs

Blazing Star, *Ladies' Art Company,* 1898

Flying Bat, *Ladies' Art Company,* 1898
Dove in the Window, Formosa Tea Leaf, Four Doves, Harvest Sun

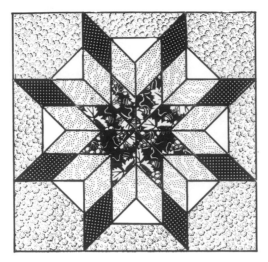

Patty's Star, *The Romance of the Patchwork Quilt in America,* 1935

Virginia Star, *101 Patchwork Patterns,* 1931
Harvest Sun, Prairie Star, Ship's Wheel

Stars upon Stars, *Ladies' Art Company,* 1898

Peony Block, *Ladies' Art Company,* 1898

Forbidden Fruit Tree, *Ladies' Art Company,* 1898

Flower Pot, *Practical Needlework,* ca. 1910
Calico Bush, Tulip Basket

Flying Swallows, *Ladies' Art Company,* 1898
Circling Swallow, Falling Star, Flying Star, Flying Swallow, Whirling Star, Wreath

Fish, Whirligig, *Practical Needlework,* ca. 1910
Airplanes, Dove in the Window, Fish Block, Gold Fish, Trout and Bass Block

Morning Star, Evening Star, *The Romance of the Patchwork Quilt in America,* 1935
Spiderweb

Star Bright, by Jinny Beyer, 1977

Eight-Pointed Star Designs

The Priscilla, *Ladies' Art Company,* 1898
Crazy Quilt Star, Diamond and Star, Kaleidoscopic Patch, World Without End

Ladies' Beautiful Star, *Ladies' Art Company,* 1898
Beautiful Star, Fancy Star

Patchwork Design, *The Ladies' Friend,* 1866
Blazing Star, Eight-Pointed Stars, Four-Pointed Star, Mother's Delight

Double Star, by Lesly-Claire Greenberg, 1979

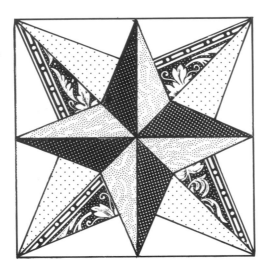

Western Spy, *Practical Needlework,* ca. 1910

Star of Empire, *Practical Needlework,* ca. 1910

Eight-Pointed Star Designs

Whirling Star, *Virginia Snow Patchwork Designs,* ca. 1930

Enigma, *Ladies' Art Company,* 1898

Star of North Carolina, *Ladies' Art Company,* 1922

Godey Design, *Godey's Lady's Book,* 1851, **Castle Wall**

Castle Keep, by Jinny Beyer, 1979

Fortress, by Jinny Beyer, 1980

Eight-Pointed Star Designs

Harlequin, by Jinny Beyer, 1980

Court Jester, by Jinny Beyer, 1980

Courtyard Square, by Jinny Beyer, 1980

Venetian Design, *Ladies' Art Company,* 1898

Interlocked Square, *Kansas City Star,* 1932

Kansas Dust Storm, *Kansas City Star,* 1935

Eight-Pointed Star Designs

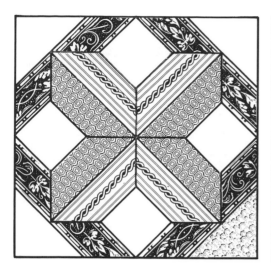

Shaded Trail, *Kansas City Star,* 1935

Godey Design, *Godey's Lady's Book,* 1852

Wandering Jew, *Practical Needlework,* ca. 1910

Wood Lily, Indian Head, *Kansas City Star,* 1936

Starlight, *Ladies' Art Company,* 1928

Rolling Star, *Ladies' Art Company,* 1898
Brunswick Star

111

Eight-Pointed Star Designs

Blazing Star, *Kansas City Star,* 1930

Star and Chains, *Ladies' Art Company,* 1898
Chained Star, Ring around the Star

Square A, *Hearth and Home,* 1870
Broken Star, Carpenter Wheel, Double Star, Dutch Rose, Octagonal Star, Star and Diamond, Star within a Star, Unknown Star

Star of Bethlehem, *The Romance of the Patchwork Quilt in America,* 1935
Star of Magi

Star Patchwork, *Farm and Home,* 1890
Captive Beauty, Cubes and Tile, Heavenly Stars, Maple Leaf, Stars and Cubes, Snow Crystals

Dutch Rose, *Practical Needlework,* ca. 1910

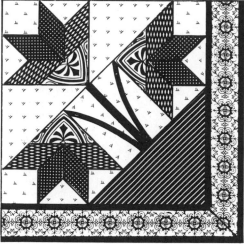

Double Peony, *Ladies' Art Company,* 1898
Triple Sunflower

Basket of Lilies, *Ladies' Art Company,* 1898
North Carolina Lily, Royal Japanese Vase

Star of Many Points, *Ladies' Art Company,* 1898
Arrowhead Star, Laurel Wreath, Welcome Hand

Lily, by Lesly-Claire Greenberg, 1979

Goose Tracks, *Ladies' Art Company,* 1898
Cross and Crown, Crossroads, Duck Paddle, Fanny's Fan, Flying Darts, Lilies

Kaleidoscope, *Virginia Snow Patchwork Designs,* ca. 1930

113

Eight-Pointed Star Designs

Directions, by Judy Spahn, 1979

Shamrock, by Jinny Beyer, 1978. Both an eight-pointed star and nine-patch grid are needed for this design.

Dutch Blades, by Jinny Beyer, 1978. Eight-pointed star and 16 square, four-patch grids are needed to make this.

HEXAGON DESIGNS

The Columbia, antique quilt, ca. 1920.

Hexagon Designs

Honeycomb, Six-sided or
Hexagon Patchwork,
Godey's Lady's Book, 1835
**Grandmother's Flower
Garden**

Field of Diamonds

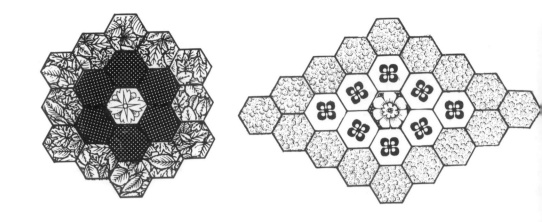

A Hexagon, *Ladies' Art
Company,* 1898

Spider Web, *Grandmother
Clark's Authentic Early
American Quilts,* 1932

Six-Pointed Star, *Practical
Needlework,* ca. 1910
Hexagonal Star, Rising Star

Block Star, *Virginia Snow
Patchwork Designs,*
ca. 1930

Hexagon Designs

Texas Star, *Ladies' Art Company*, 1922

Spinning Star, by Jinny Beyer, 1979

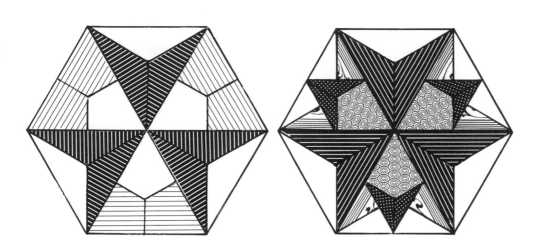

Bows and Arrows, by Jinny Beyer, 1979

Arrowhead Star, by Jinny Beyer, 1979

Eastern Star, by Jinny Beyer, 1979

Asteroid, by Jinny Beyer, 1979

117

Hexagon Designs

Colonial Garden, *Grand-mother Clark's Authentic Early American Quilts,* 1932

Colorado Star, by Jinny Beyer, 1979

Madison Quilt Block, *Ladies' Art Company,* 1922

Starry Nights, by Alice Newton, 1979

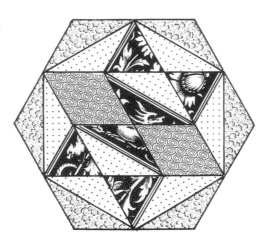

Block Patchwork, *Ladies' Art Company,* 1898

The Columbia, *Ladies' Art Company,* 1898

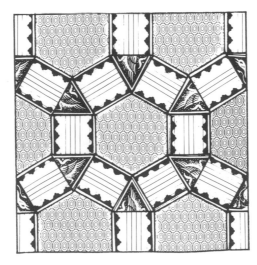
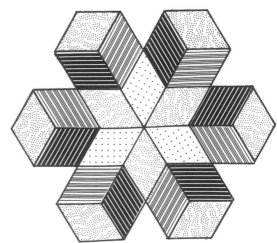

Hexagon Designs

Godey Design, *Godey's Lady's Book,* 1851
Cube Work, Baby Blocks, Building Blocks, Cubes and Stars, Diamond Cube, Tumbling Blocks, Variegated Diamonds

Godey Design, *Godey's Lady's Book,* 1851
Brick Pile

Right Angle Patchwork, *Dictionary of Needlework,* 1882
Ecclesiastical, Inner City

CURVED DESIGNS

Sunflower, detail of quilt of Indian cottons, by Jinny Beyer.
Photograph by Steve Thompson.

SECTION 1: CURVED DESIGNS BASED ON ANOTHER GRID

FOUR SQUARE FOUR-PATCH

Orange Peel, *Ladies' Art Company,* 1898
Lafayette Orange Peel, Melon Patch

Pin Cushion, *Ladies' Art Company,* 1898
Robbing Peter to Pay Paul

Greek Square, *Ladies' Art Company,* 1898

16 SQUARE FOUR-PATCH

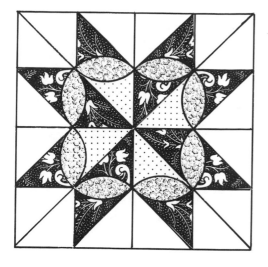

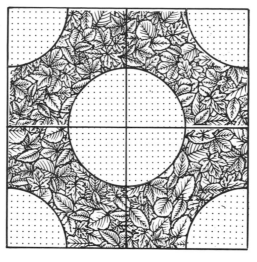

Winding Walk, *Ladies' Art Company,* 1898
Biloxi, Fox Chase

Baseball, *Ladies Art Company,* 1898
Robbing Peter to Pay Paul

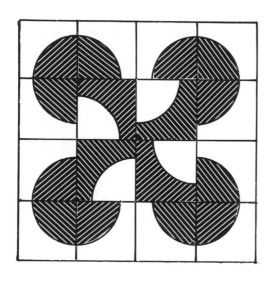

Fool's Puzzle, *Ladies' Art Company,* 1898
Wonder of the World

Drunkard's Path, *Ladies' Art Company,* 1898
Country Husband, Drunkard's Trail, Rocky Road to California, Rocky Road to Dublin

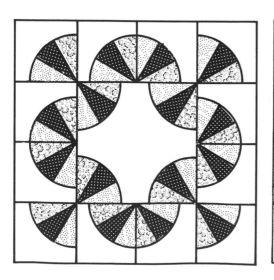

Mohawk Trail, *Virginia Snow Patchwork Designs,* ca. 1930

Baby Bunting, *Ladies' Art Company,* 1928

64 SQUARE FOUR-PATCH

Mill Wheel, *101 Patchwork Patterns,* 1931
Snowball

Fair Play, *Ladies' Art Company,* 1922

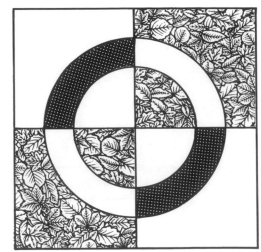

Hearts and Gizzards,
Ladies' Art Company, 1898
**Lazy Daisy, Petal Quilt,
Springtime Blossoms,
Wheel of Fortune**

Pullman Puzzle, *Ladies'
Art Company,* 1898
Baseball

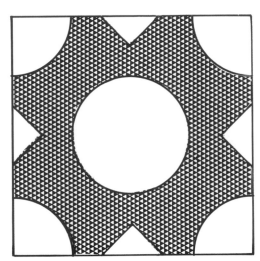

Homecoming by Yoko
Sawanobori, 1979

Hearts Design, *Kansas City
Star,* 1932
Little Giant

Curved Designs

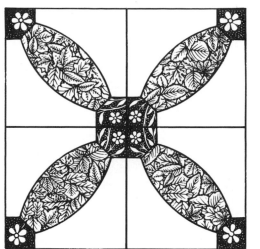

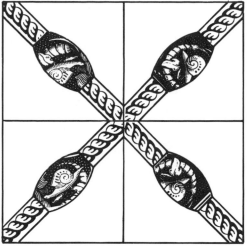

Whale Block, *Ladies' Art Company,* 1922

The Snail's Trail, *Ladies' Art Company,* 1898

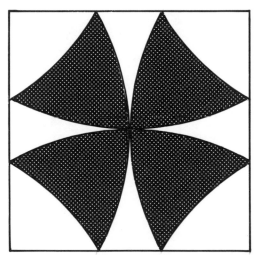

Winding Ways, *Ladies' Art Company,* 1922
Four Leaf Clover, Wheel of Mystery

Cockleburr, *Ladies' Art Company,* 1928

Philadelphia Patch, *Ladies' Art Company,* 1922

NINE SQUARE NINE-PATCH

Tea Leaf, *Ladies' Art Company,* 1898
Bay Leaf, Lover's Knot

Wings, *Ladies' Art Company,* 1928

Lock and Chain, *Ladies' Art Company,* 1922
Amethyst Chain

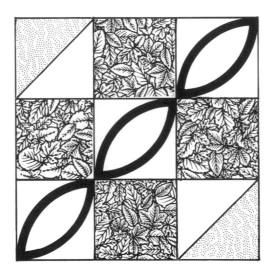

Curved Designs

Greek Cross, *Ladies' Art Company,* 1898

Trenton Quilt Block, *Ladies' Art Company,* 1922

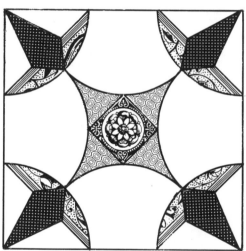

The Royal, *Ladies' Art Company,* 1898
Royal Cross, Tennessee Circle

Swinging Corners, *Ladies' Art Company,* 1898
Swallow's Nest

Love Ring, *The Romance of the Patchwork Quilt in America,* 1935

Bleeding Heart, *Ladies' Art Company,* 1928

Curved Designs

Milwaukee's Own, *Ladies' Art Company,* 1922

Dover Quilt Block, *Ladies' Art Company,* 1922

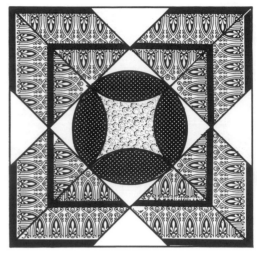

Godey Design, *Godey's Lady's Book,* 1857
Martha's Choice, Virginia's Choice

Orange Peel, *Virginia Snow Patchwork Designs,* ca. 1930

Chimney Swallows, *Ladies' Art Company,* 1898
Coronation, King's Crown, Potomac's Pride, President's Quilt

Polaris, by Sandy Tucker, 1979

Old Maid's Combination,
Ladies' Art Company, 1898
Square and Compass

SEVEN-PATCH CURVED DESIGNS

Fox and Geese, *Ladies' Art Company,* 1922

Queen's Crown, *Ladies' Art Company,* 1922
Chinese Fan, Cleopatra's Puzzle

Ladies' Fancy, *The Farm and Fireside,* 1884

Four Little Baskets, *Ladies' Art Company,* 1898

129

EIGHT-POINTED STAR CURVED DESIGNS

French Star, *101 Patchwork Patterns,* 1931
Gleaming Sun

The King's Crown, *Ladies' Art Company,* 1898
King's Star

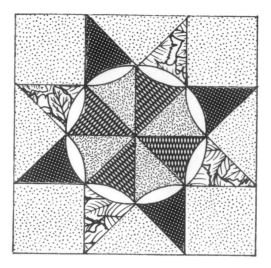 

Twinkling Stars, *Ladies' Art Company,* 1898
Celestial Sphere

The Four Winds, *Kansas City Star,* 1932
Alaska Chinook, Compass, Star and Crescent, Star of the West

Compass, *Quilting,* 1934

SECTION 2: CURVED DESIGNS BASED ON DIVISIONS OF THE CIRCLE

The following designs are formed by dividing a circle in various ways. Rather than group them according to the number of divisions, which are easy to count, I have arranged similar designs together.

Sunflower, *Virginia Snow Patchwork Designs,* ca. 1930
Aster

Chrysanthemum, *Ladies' Art Company,* 1898
Dresden Plate

Star of the West, Union Star, *Ladies' Art Company,* 1898

Savannah Beautiful Star, *Ladies' Art Company,* 1922

Cog Wheels, *Ladies' Art Company,* 1898

Wheel of Fortune, date unknown

Curved Designs

Rising Sun, *Ladies' Art Company,* 1898
Cog Wheel

Pyrotechnics, *Ladies' Art Company,* 1898

Georgetown Circle, *Ladies' Art Company,* 1898

Single Sunflower, *Ladies' Art Company,* 1898
Blazing Star

Wild Flower, by Judy Spahn, 1979

Sunflower, Sunburst, *Practical Needlework,* ca. 1910

132

Curved Designs

Oklahoma Sunburst, *Kansas City Star,* 1931

Himalayan Sun, by Jinny Beyer, 1979

Fortune's Wheel, *Ladies' Art Company,* 1928

Sunflower

Slashed Star, *Ladies' Art Company,* 1898
Blazing Star, Blazing Sun, Chips and Whetstones, Mariner's Compass, Sunflower

Sunburst, *Ladies' Home Journal,* 1908
Mariner's Compass

Curved Designs

Godey Design, *Godey's Lady's Book,* 1858

Wyoming Patch, *Ladies' Art Company,* 1928

Godey Design, *Godey's Lady's Book,* 1858

The Sunflower, *Ladies' Art Company,* 1898

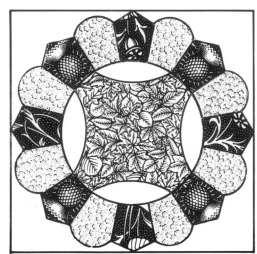

Harrison Rose, *Quilts, Their Story and How to Make Them,* 1915

Strawberry, *Ladies' Art Company,* 1898
Friendship Ring, Full Blown Tulip, Oriental Star

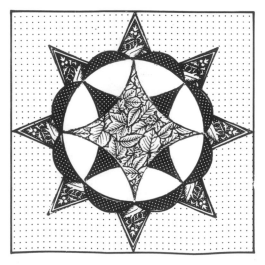

Curved Designs

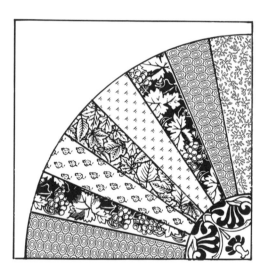

Victoria's Crown, *Grandmother Clark's Authentic Early American Quilts,* 1932

Mary's Fan, *Virginia Snow Patchwork Designs,* ca. 1930

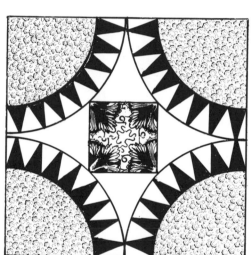

Fan Patchwork, *Ladies' Art Company,* 1898
Grandmother's Fan

Suspension Bridge, *Ladies' Art Company,* 1922
Broken Circle, Indian Summer, Sunflower

Double Wedding Ring, *Ladies' Art Company,* 1928

Indian Wedding Ring, *Grandmother Clark's Authentic Early American Patchwork Quilts,* 1932

135

ISOLATED SQUARE DESIGNS

Log Cabin, antique quilt of calicoes, ca. 1875. Photograph by Steve Thompson.

Isolated Square Designs

Pineapple, detail of quilt, ca. 1900. Owned by Dick and Ellen Swanson.
Photograph by Steve Thompson.

Log House Quilting, *Dictionary of Needlework,* 1882
Log Cabin, American Log Patchwork, The Log Patch

Courthouse Steps

Pineapple, *Ladies' Art Company,* 1898

King David's Crown, *The Romance of the Patchwork Quilt in America,* 1935

Mexican Star, *101 Patchwork Patterns,* 1931
Dallas Star, Mexican Rose, Panama Block

Ray of Light, medallion quilt, by Jinny Beyer.

BORDERS

As quiltmakers become more innovative, they seek ways to enhance both traditional and original designs. This quest, coupled with the surge of interest in medallion quilts, has created a need for border designs which go beyond the traditional sawtooth, dog tooth, diamond, or square borders. For this reason, I have presented a large group of border designs which can be used in various aspects of quiltmaking.

Some of the borders included are traditional patterns; others have been created by quiltmakers whose names appear below their design. Most, however, are ones I have devised by looking at many of the old designs and working with the shapes until I developed a border I liked. They are classified into squares and triangles, hexagons, eight-pointed stars and curves. A design that has any curves will go into the curve section regardless of how it is otherwise drafted.

The borders based on squares and triangles are actually drafted on grids that are composed of a certain number of squares. Grids have been drawn at one end of each design to show how they have been drafted. These borders, using a grid of one, two, three, or four squares, have been sorted into groups. There are some that require even more squares, but they will be apparent when you study the grids.

Borders based on the eight-pointed star and hexagon cannot be drafted on a grid of squares. These two configurations must be drafted separately before they can be used in the border design.

One of the most difficult parts in designing a border is planning how to turn the corners. If the border does not flow smoothly at this point, it can affect the overall look of the entire quilt. A border should never just stop at any old place and start up again around the corner. To be appealing to the eye it must provide a symmetrical frame around the the quilt.

Because I feel the corners are so important, I have shown how every border can be made to turn a corner gracefully. Each of the designs, therefore, includes a straight strip and one corner.

In order for the corners to be symmetrical, it is often necessary to reverse the direction of the border at some point. For example, the corner of a sawtooth border that has all the triangles going in the same direction looks awkward.

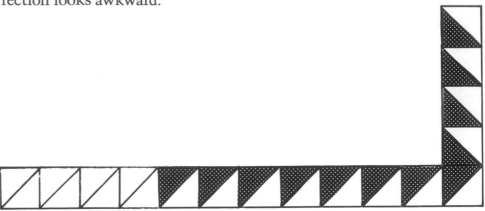

When working with a design like this, I prefer to reverse the direction of the pieces at the mid-point of the border strip. By doing this on all four sides of a quilt, the corners will be symmetrical. Sometimes the *design* does not need to be reversed, but just the coloring.

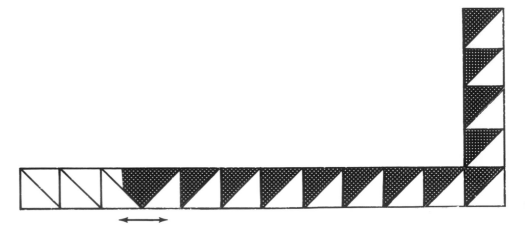

In the following border illustrations, I have reversed the direction of those borders that need it in order to achieve uniform corners. Each of those borders has arrows at the place where the border has been reversed.

It is very difficult to turn the corner effectively when using a hexagon border design. The only way I know of to do it uniformly is to *miter* the design at each corner.

The border designs presented here are only a beginning. The possibilities are unlimited! If none seems suitable for enhancing your quilt, experiment with the shapes of your quilt design until a border emerges that pleases you.

ONE SQUARE GRID BORDERS

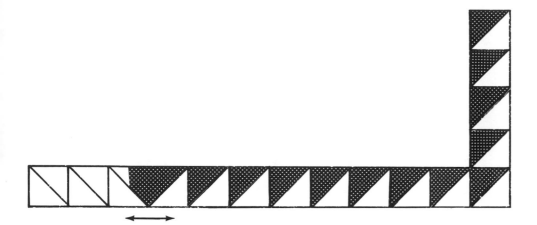

Sawtooth

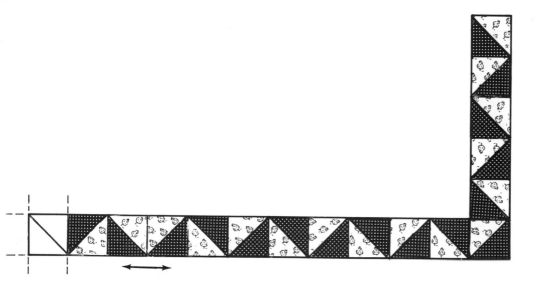

Reverse Sawtooth

Ribbon Twist

144

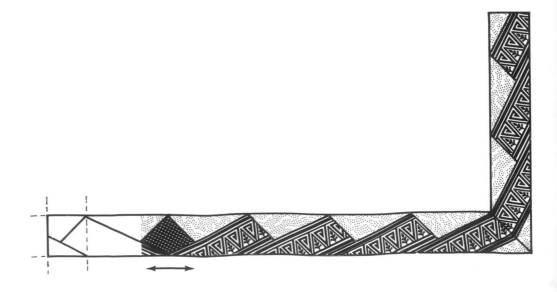

TWO SQUARE GRID BORDERS

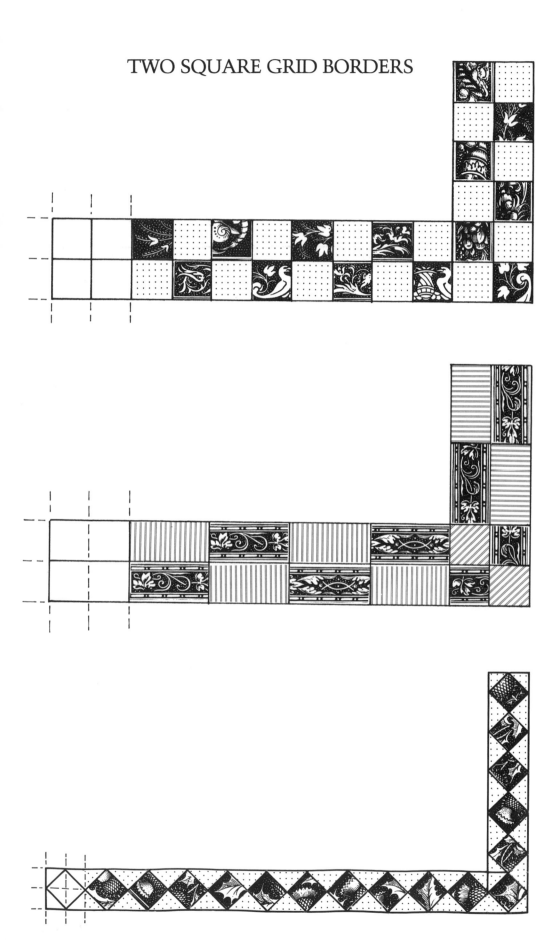

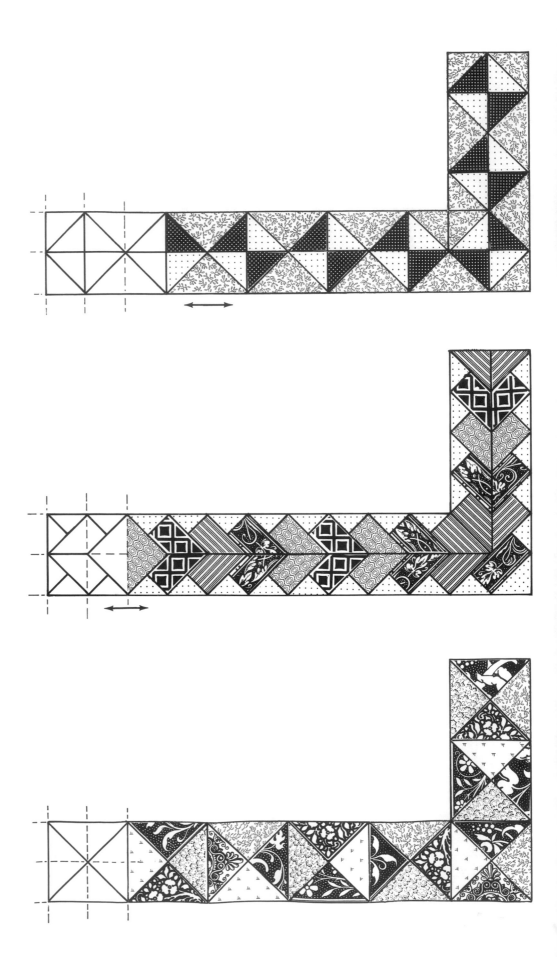

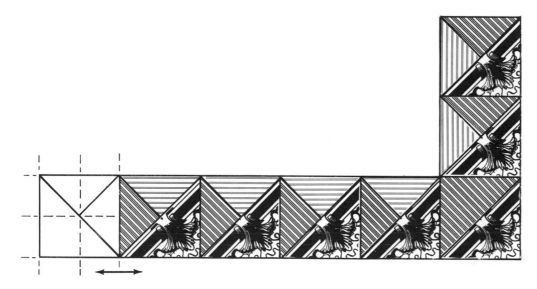

Air Castle

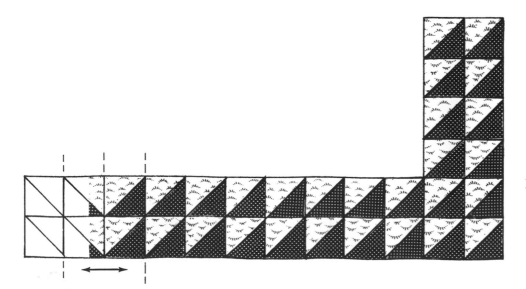

Double Sawtooth

Borders

Wild Goose Chase
Ladies' Art Company, 1898

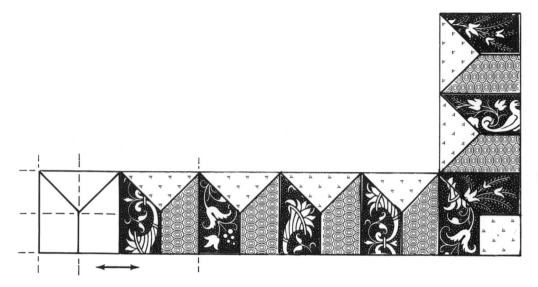

Nelson's Victory

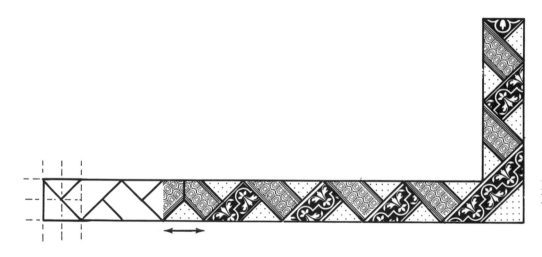

Folded Ribbon, by Nancy
Nelson, 1979

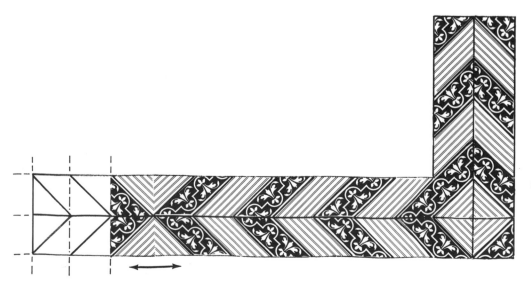

Chevron

149

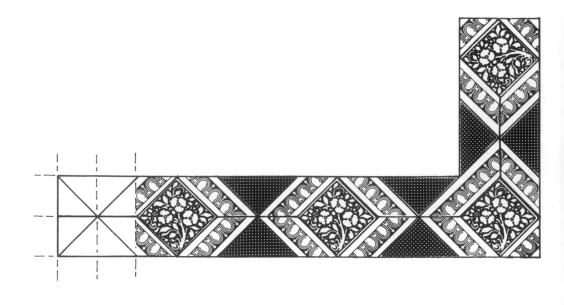

Double Ribbon Twist

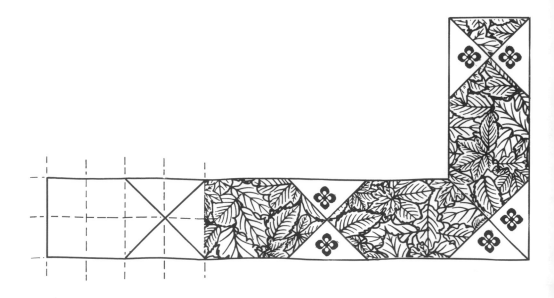

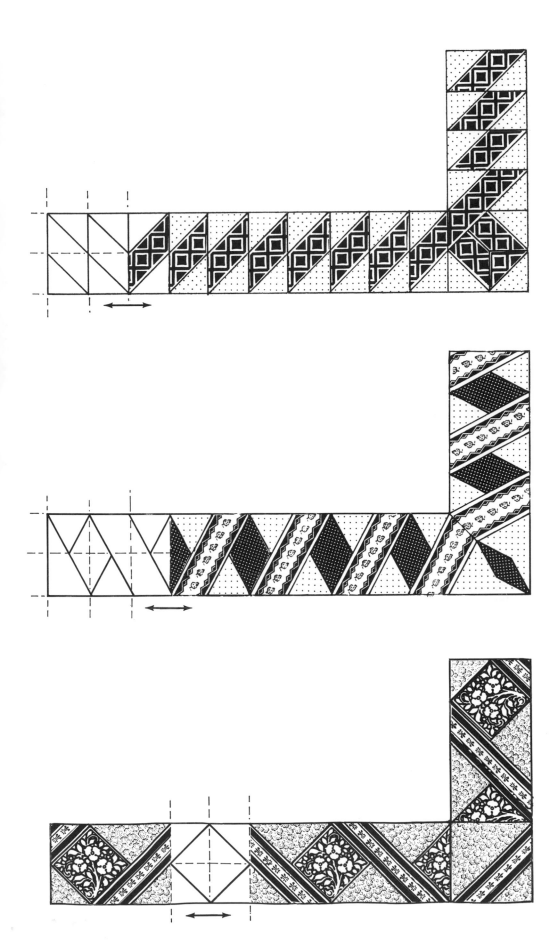

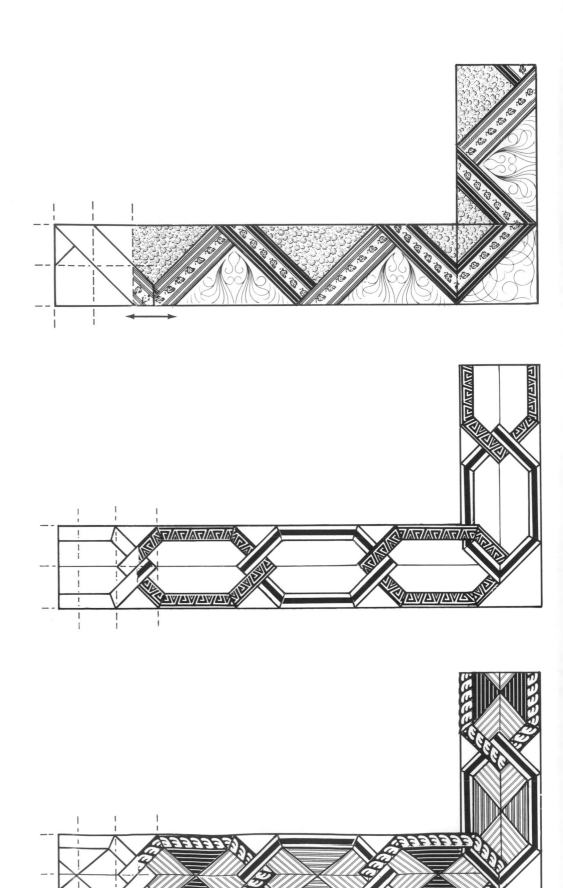

Tibetan Panel, by Jinny Beyer, 1979

Dog Tooth

153

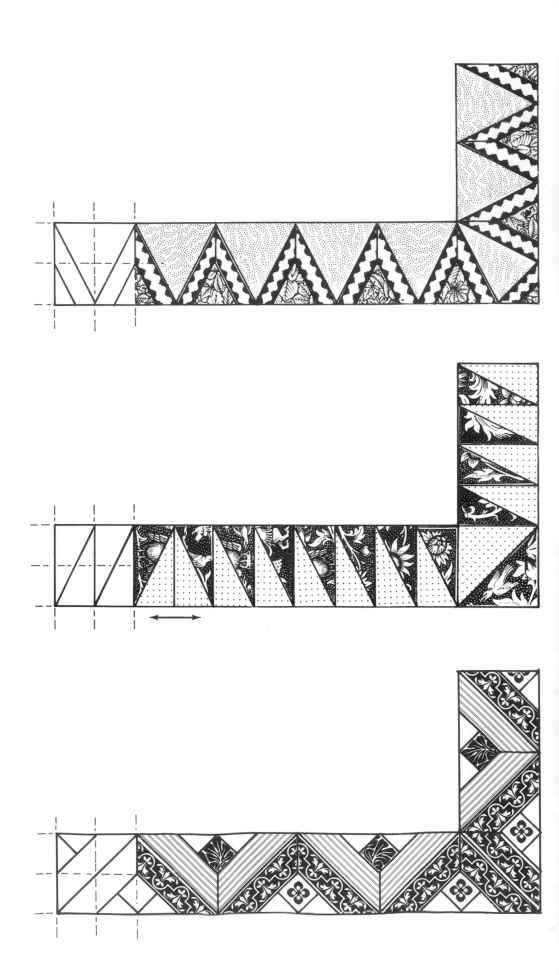

THREE SQUARE GRID BORDERS

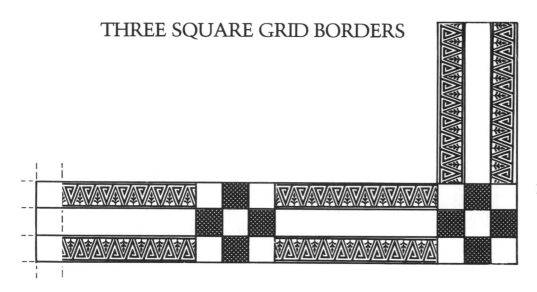

Nine-Patch Border

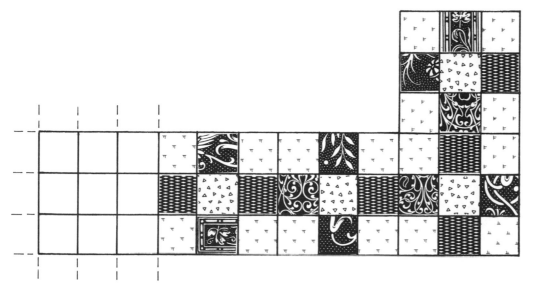

Nine-Patch Border

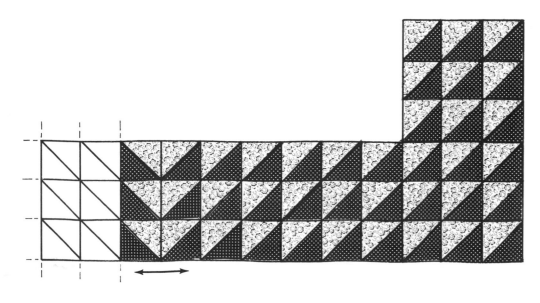

Triple Sawtooth

Borders

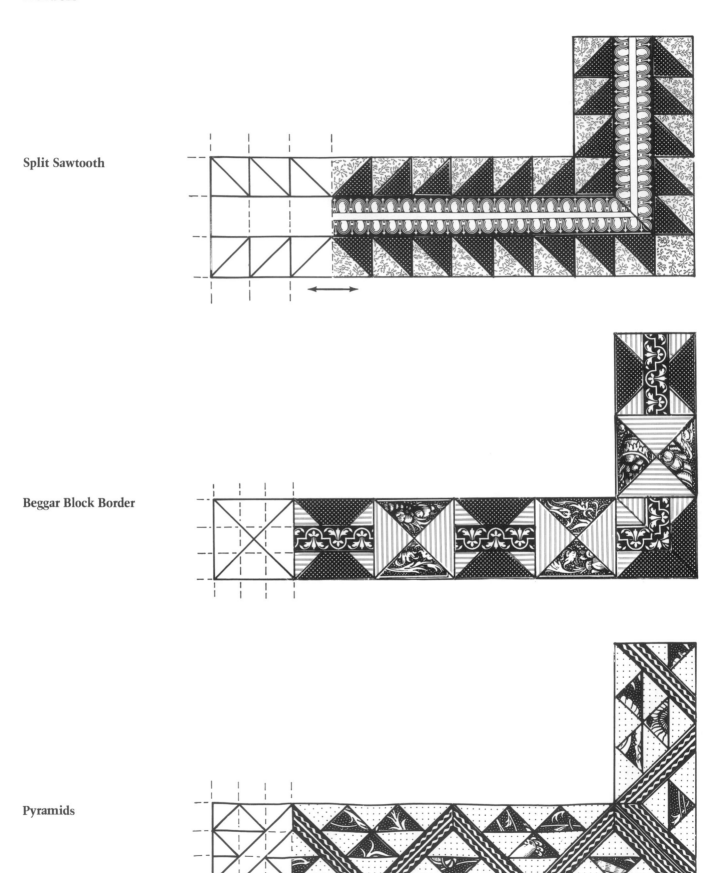

Split Sawtooth

Beggar Block Border

Pyramids

156

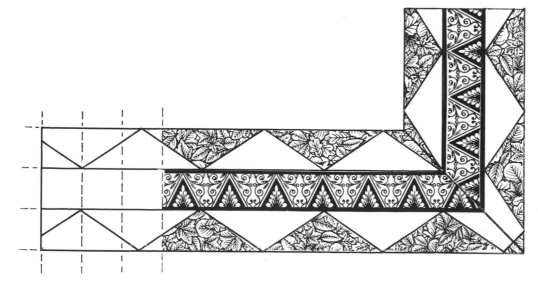

Joseph's Coat Border

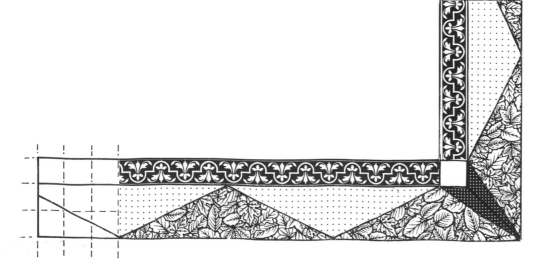

Border Design, by Barbara
Bockman, 1980

157

Borders

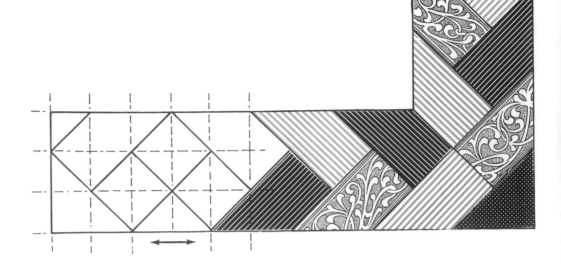

Peterson Design Border,
*Peterson's Ladies'
Magazine,* 1884

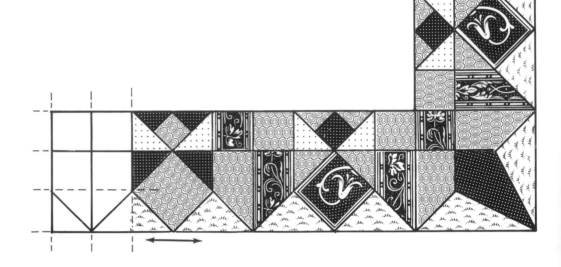

Seattle Sights Border, by
Alice Newton, 1979

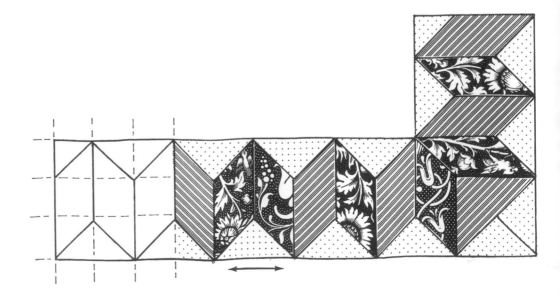

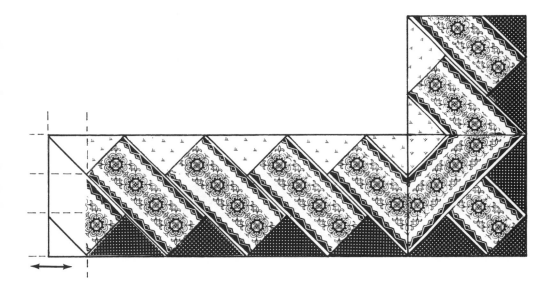

Aunt Eliza's Star Border

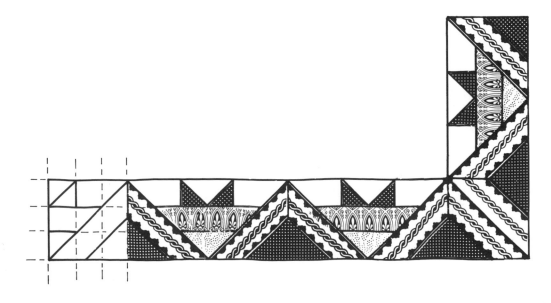

Borders

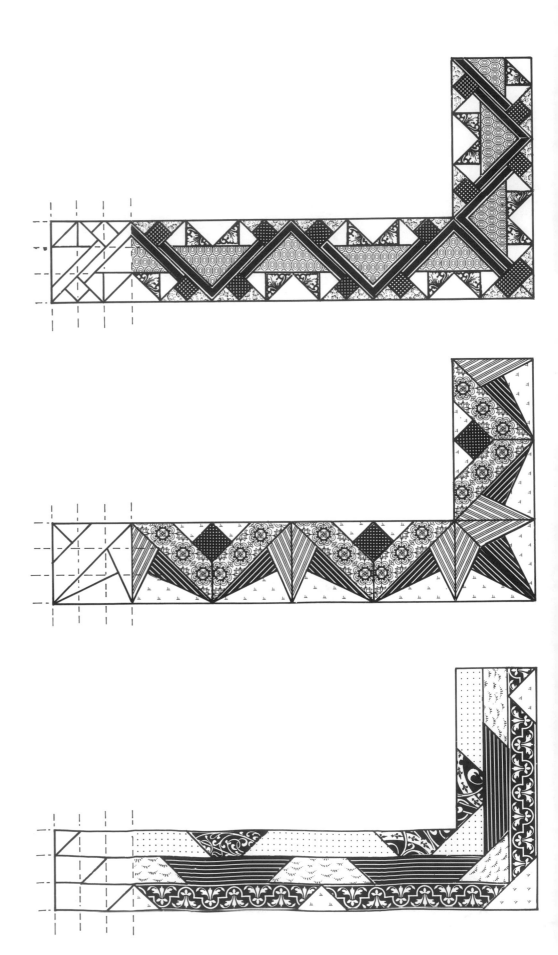

Grandmother's Cross Border, by Marjorie Jung, 1980

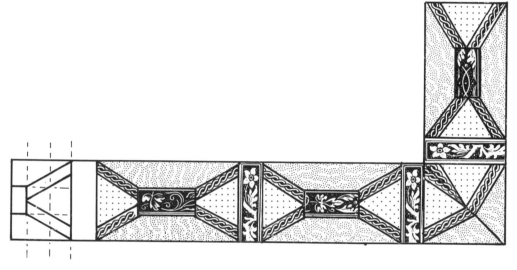

Godey Design, *Godey's Lady's Book,* 1858

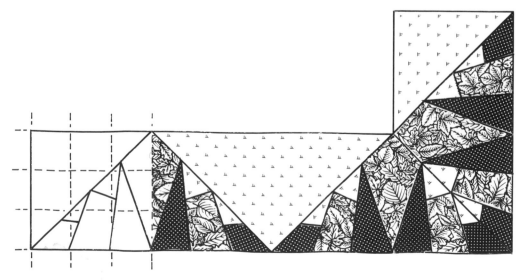

Poinsettia Border, by Fay Goldey, 1979

161

Borders

Square within Square Border

162

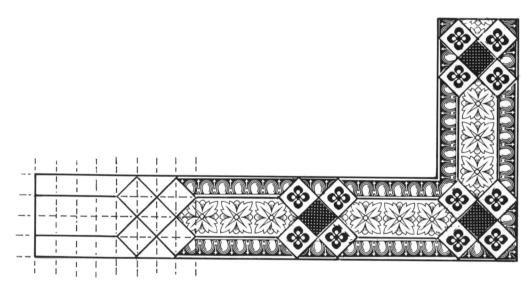

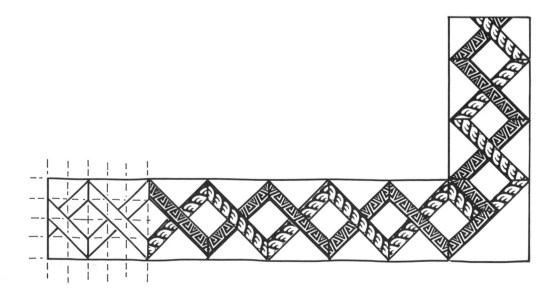

Borders

Lattice Border, by Patt
Madlener, 1978

Border Design, by Barbara
Bockman, 1980

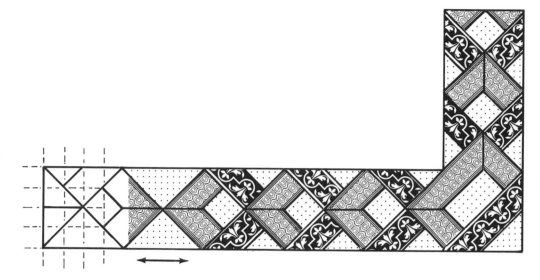

Double Folded Ribbon, by
Nancy Nelson, 1979

Border Design, by Sandy
Tucker, 1979

Border Design, by Barbara
Bockman, 1980

Borders

Ribbon Border, *Ladies' Art Company,* 1898

Border Design, by Virginia Suzuki

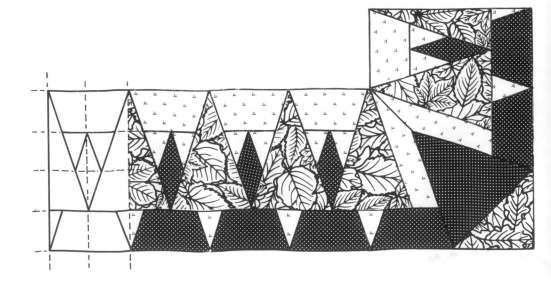

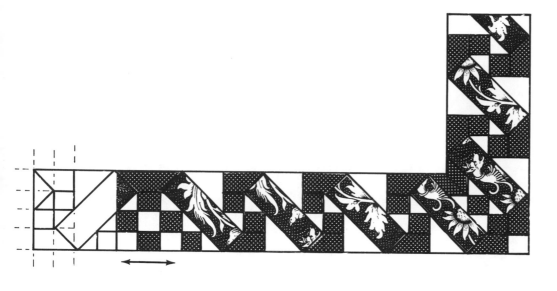

Border Design, by Patt
Madlener, 1978

Borders

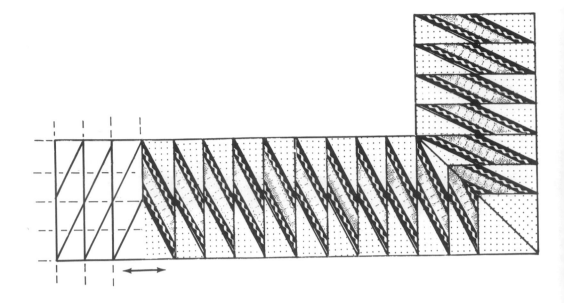

Godey Design, *Godey's Lady's Book,* 1858

MULTIPLE GRID BORDERS

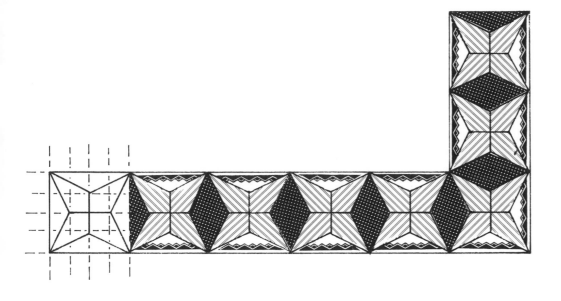

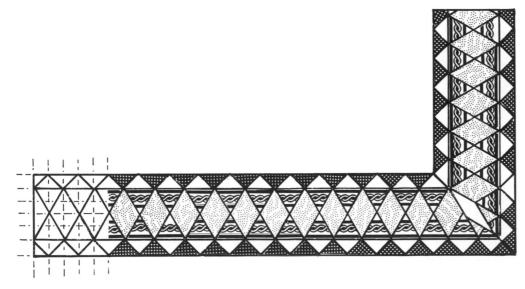

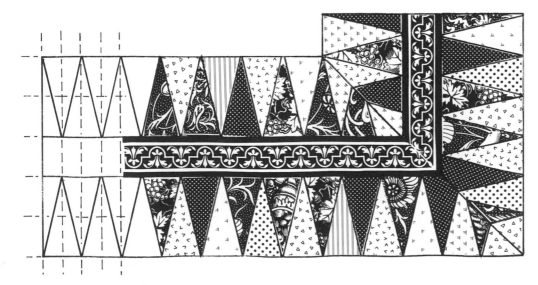

Double Dog Tooth

171

Borders

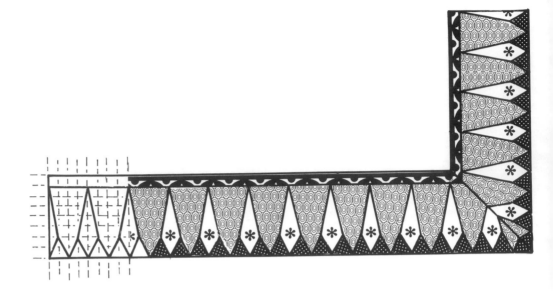

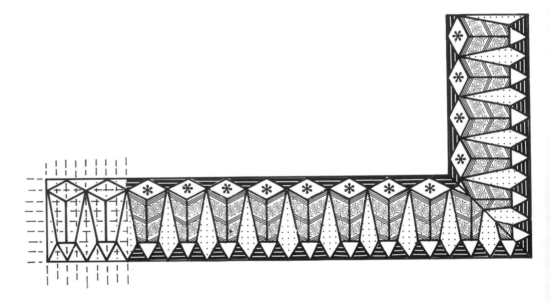

Mariner's Compass Border,
by Alice Newton, 1979

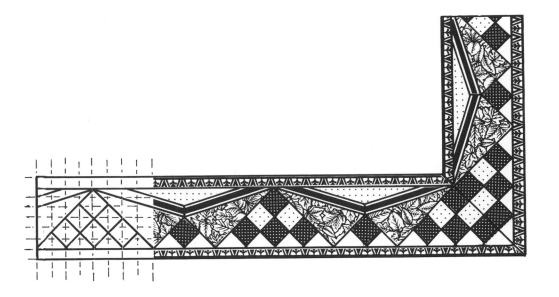

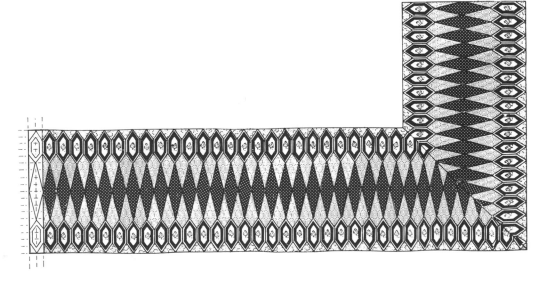

173

HEXAGON BORDERS

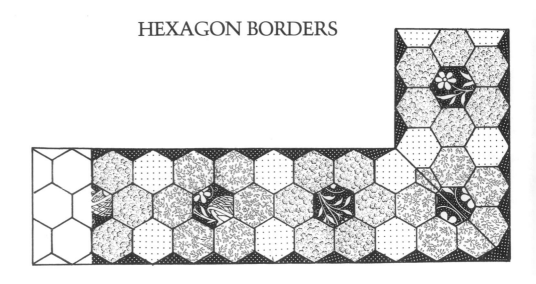

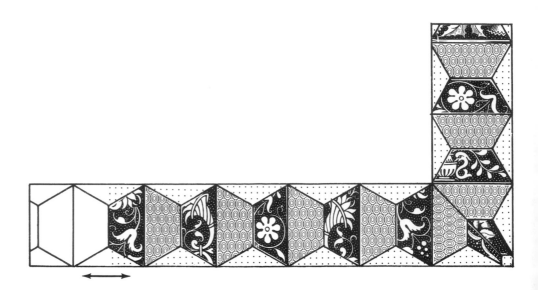

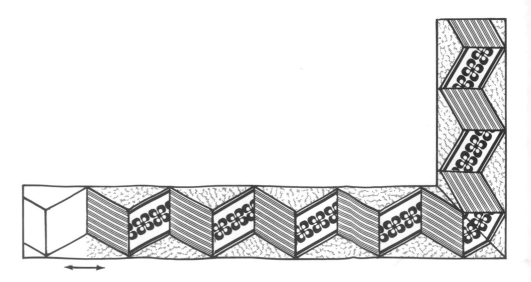

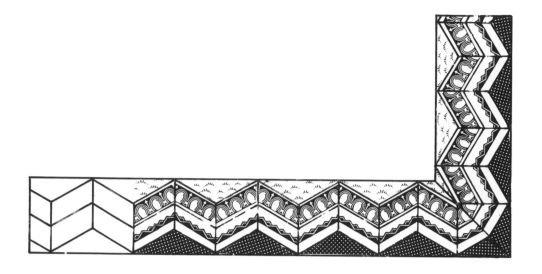

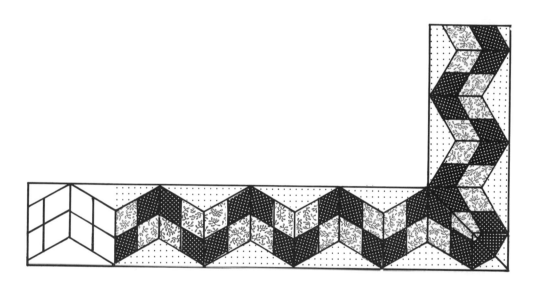

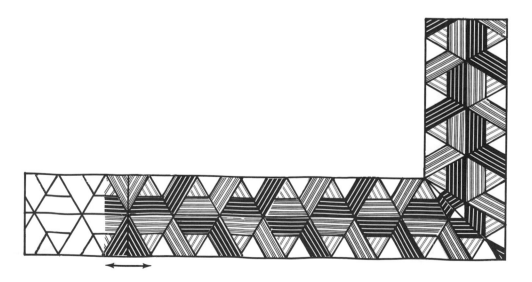

Borders

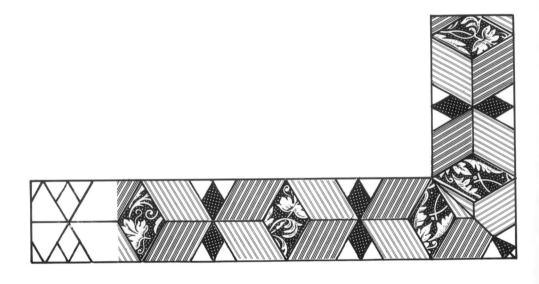

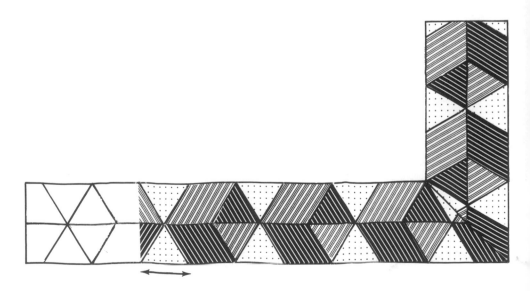

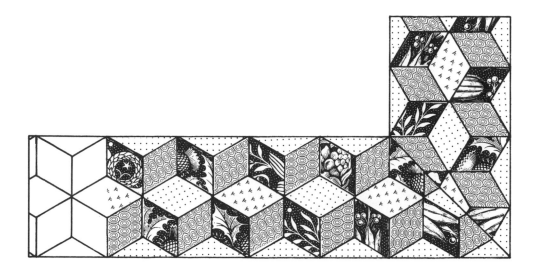

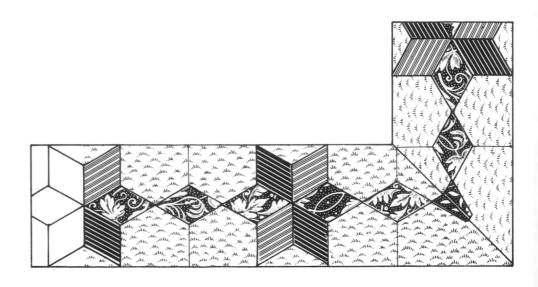

EIGHT-POINTED STAR BORDERS

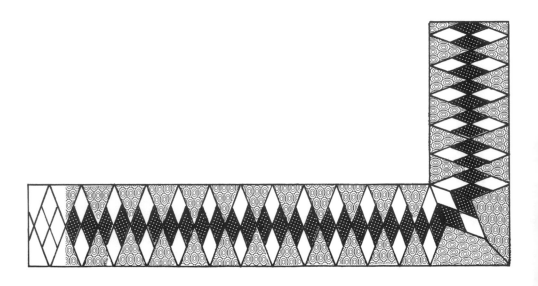

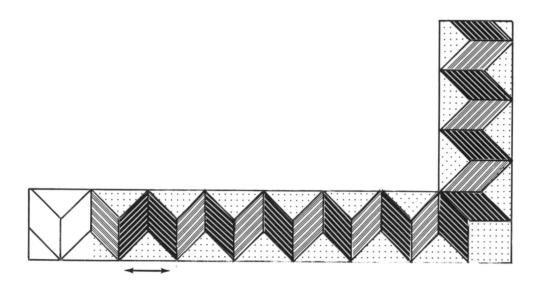

Star of Bethlehem Border

Borders

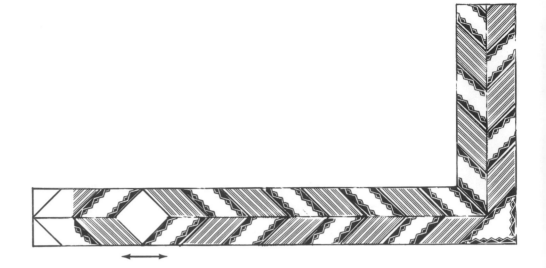

Wood Lily Border

Turkey Tracks Border

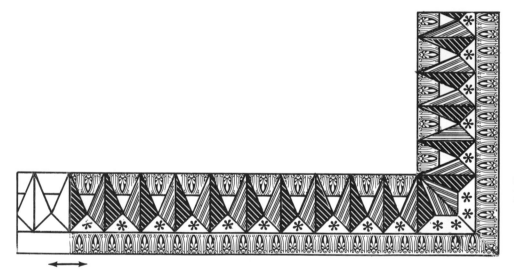

Castle Keep Border, by
Jinny Beyer, 1980

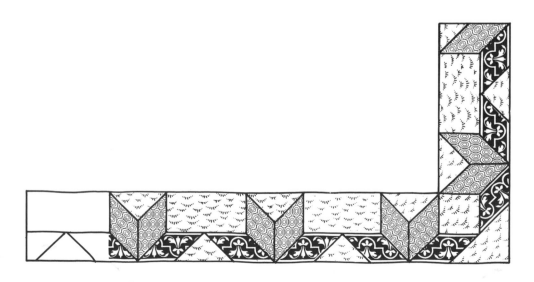

Borders

Castle Wall Border

Border Design, by Dan
Ramsey, 1980

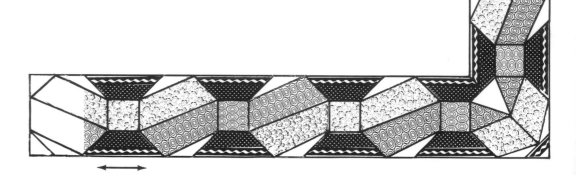

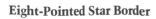

Eight-Pointed Star Border

Octagon Border

CURVED BORDERS

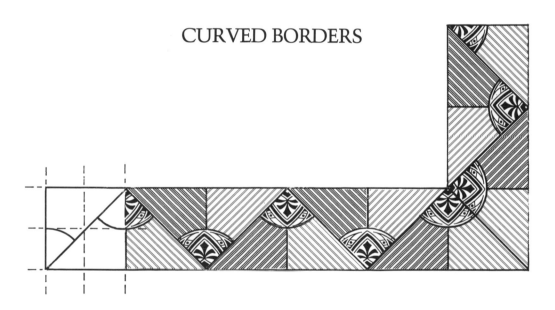

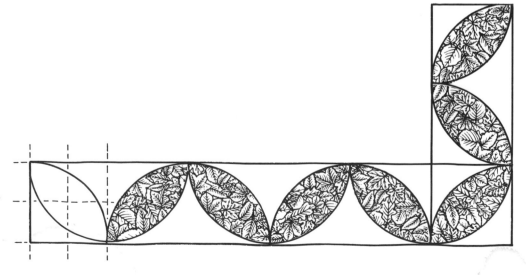

Orange Peel Border

Borders

Double Wedding Ring Border

Pickle Dish, Indian Wedding Ring Border

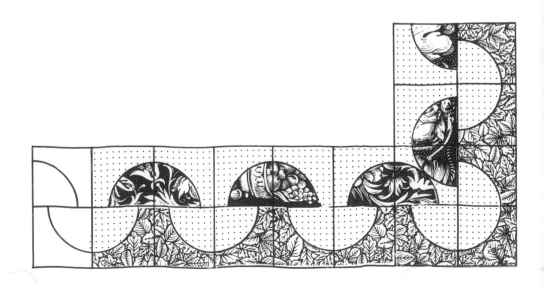

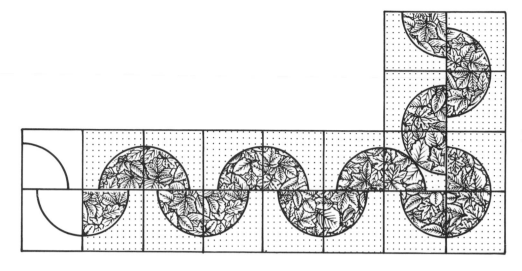

Drunkard's Path Border

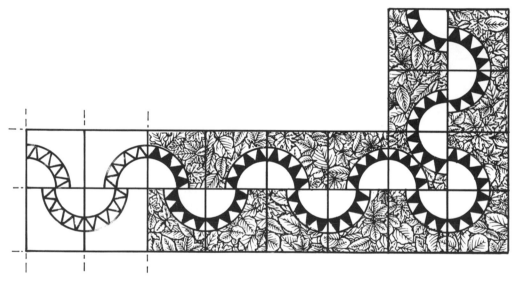

Baby Bunting Border, by Eleanor Kastner, 1979

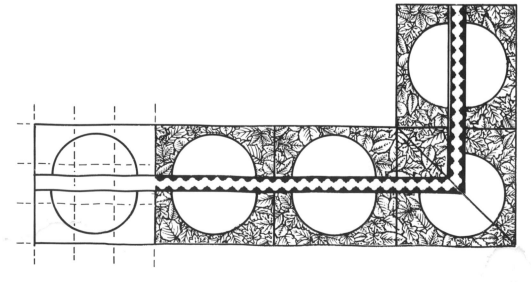

Drunkard's Path Border, by Alice Newton, 1979

Borders

Mohawk Trail Border

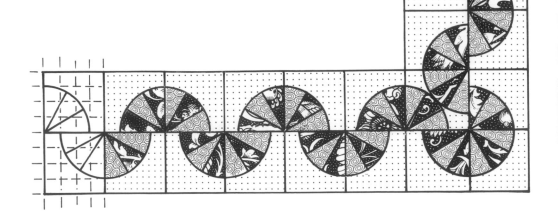

Dresden Plate Border

Border Design, by
Marilyn Titman, 1979

Sunflower Border

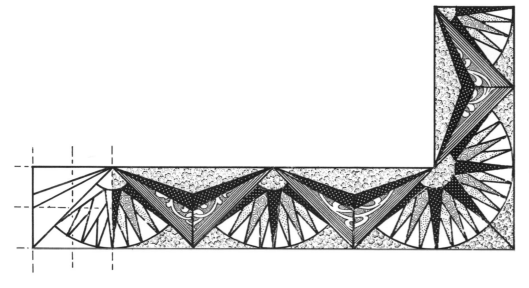

Mariner's Compass Border

Blazing Star Border

BIBLIOGRAPHY

Beyer, Alice. *Quilting*. Chicago, Illinois: South Park Commissioners, 1934. Reprinted by the East Bay Heritage Quilters, Albany, California, 1978.

Beyer, Jinny. *Patchwork Patterns*. McLean, Virginia: EPM Publications, Inc., 1979.

Caulfield, S.F.A. and Saward, Blanche C. *The Dictionary of Needlework, An Encyclopedia of Artistic, Plain, and Fancy Needlework*. London: L. Upcott Gill, 1882.

Colby, Averil. *Patchwork*. London: B. T. Batsford Ltd., 1958.

Farm and Fireside. Springfield, Ohio: Crowell Publishing Co., 1884.

The Farmers Wife Book of Quilts. St. Paul, Minnesota: Webb Publishing Co., 1931.

Finley, Ruth E. *Old Patchwork Quilts and the Women Who Made Them*. Philadelphia: J. B. Lippincott Company, 1929.

Frank Leslie's Modenwelt, New York: Frank Leslie Co., 1870.

Frost, S. Annie. *The Ladies' Guide to Needlework, Embroidery, etc.*, 1877.

Godey's Lady's Book. New York: The Godey Company, 1830-1898.

Grandmother Clark's Authentic Early American Patchwork Quilts. St. Louis, Missouri: WLM Clark Inc., 1932.

Gutcheon, Beth. *The Perfect Patchwork Primer*. Westford, Massachusetts: David McKay Company, Inc., 1973. Published in Penguin Books, 1974.

Gutcheon, Beth and Jeffrey. *The Quilt Design Workbook*. New York: Rawson Associates Publishers, Inc., 1976.

Hall, Carrie A. and Kretsinger, Rose G. *The Romance of the Patchwork Quilt in America*. New York: The Caxton Printers, Ltd., 1935.

Hearth and Home Newspapers. New York: Pettengill, Bates and Co., 1868-1875.

The Home Magazine. Minneapolis: P. V. Colling Publishing Co., 1891.

Ickis, Marguerite. *The Standard Book of Quiltmaking and Collecting*. Greystone Press, 1949. Republished, New York: Dover Publications, Inc., 1959.

The Kansas City Star Newspapers. Kansas City: 1925-1945.

Ladies Art Company Catalogue. St. Louis, Missouri: Ladies Art Company, 1898, 1922, 1928.

The Ladies Home Journal. Philadelphia: Curtis Publishing Company, 1896-1910.

McKim, Mrs. Ruby Short. *101 Patchwork Patterns.* Independence, Missouri: McKim Studios, 1938. Reprinted by Dover Publications, 1962.

Orlofsky, Patsy and Myron. *Quilts in America.* New York: McGraw-Hill Book Company, 1974.

Peterson Magazine. New York: Penfield Publishing Co., 1843-1894.

Pullan, Mrs. *The Lady's Manual of Fancy-Work.* New York: Dick and Fitzgerald, 1859.

Quilter's Newsletter Magazine. Wheatridge, Colorado: Leman Publications, 1972-1980.

Stone, Clara A. *Practical Needlework.* Boston: C. W. Calkins and Company, ca. 1910.

Virginia Snow Patchwork Designs. Elgin, Illinois: Dexter Thread and Yarn Company, ca. 1930.

Webster, Marie D. *Quilts, Their Story and How to Make Them.* New York: Doubleday, Page and Company, 1915.

INDEX

197